Access your online resources

Promoting Physical Development and Activity in Early Childhood is accompanied by a number of printable online materials, designed to ensure this resource best supports your professional needs

Go to https://resourcecentre.routledge.com/speechmark and click on the cover of this book

Answer the question prompt using your copy of the book to gain access to the online content.

Promoting Physical Development and Activity in Early Childhood

Getting young children active and supporting their physical development right from the start is essential for children's all-round development and good health. However, children's levels of physical activity are declining. This book helps readers increase their understanding to support young children's overall development, health, and wellbeing.

Breaking current physical activity guidelines into bite-size chunks, the book provides key advice on caring for and educating babies and young children on how to meet the recommended amount of physical activity each day. Current research is accessibly explored, including links with screen time and neuroscience, and informs a range of flexible, open-ended activities and practical strategies to use in every early years setting. Chapters include:

- Suggestions on planning an enabling environment to support young children's physical development without expensive equipment or classes.
- Steps for making physical activity inclusive for all children, including those with special educational needs and physical conditions.
- Key research translated into easy-to-understand, informative guidance.
- The voice of the child and the importance of listening to children woven throughout
- Opportunities for readers to assess how their own setting supports physical activity.
- The importance of early physical development to communication and future academic performance.

Grounded in best practice for supporting physical development in the early years and working with parents, this book is essential reading for trainee and practising early years educators, as well as parents and carers of young children.

Jackie Musgrave is part of the Early Childhood team at The Open University. Jackie trained as a Registered General Nurse and then a Sick Children's Nurse, working in a range of different paediatric specialisms, including working as a Paediatric Asthma Nurse in the community. She started her teaching career in Further Education before moving into teaching Higher Education in 2005. Her research brings together her interests in children's health and early childhood education. Jackie has numerous publications related to child health and early childhood education.

Jane Dorrian joined the Early Childhood team at The Open University in 2022 after teaching on undergraduate and postgraduate courses at Cardiff Metropolitan University. She started her career as a nursery teacher in the south Wales valleys and also worked as a Local Authority advisory teacher for early years. Her research has looked at the professional identities of early childhood practitioners and she is also interested in young children's physical literacy, with her recent projects looking at how engagement in children's physical activity affects the wellbeing of parents and carers.

Joanne Josephidou is Programme Lead of the Early Childhood team at The Open University. She was a primary school teacher for many years, working predominantly in the Early Years. She has taught in both Teacher Education and on Early Childhood Studies programmes. Her research explores opportunities for babies and toddlers to engage with the outdoors and nature.

Ben Langdown is a Senior Lecturer in Sports Coaching at The Open University (The OU) and has published various papers and chapters in the areas of movement cultures, physical development, and sports science. Ben's applied interests focus on fostering a movement culture, supporting children's physical activity and development, and the application of strength and conditioning to support this. Specifically, Ben's research focuses on children's physical development, athlete monitoring, and training interventions. Alongside Ben's academic role, he also provides sports science and strength and conditioning support to young athletes. He has presented at many international conferences and delivered keynote presentations and workshops to support practitioners in various youth sports and disciplines. Further information can be found on Ben's academic profile (The OU) and by following @BenLangdown on X (Twitter).

Lucy Rodriguez Leon is a Lecturer in Early Childhood Education at The Open University. Before teaching in Higher Education, Lucy spent 16 years working at a nursery school in the east of England. Her research and publications focus on how babies and young children engage with literacies and make meaning from multimodal texts in their active play and in their everyday lives. Lucy is also interested in Early Years Workforce Development and was a member of a research team that undertook a systematic review of international research evidence on the impact of staff training and qualifications.

Little Minds Matter:

Promoting Social and Emotional Wellbeing in the Early Years

Series Advisor: Sonia Mainstone-Cotton

The *Little Minds Matter* series promotes best practice for integrating social and emotional health and wellbeing into the early years setting. It introduces practitioners to a wealth of activities and resources to support them in each key area: from providing access to ideas for unstructured, imaginative outdoor play; activities to create a sense of belonging and form positive identities; and, importantly, strategies to encourage early years professionals to create a workplace that positively contributes to their own wellbeing, as well as the quality of their provision. The *Little Minds Matter* series ensures that practitioners have the tools they need to support every child.

Building Positive Relationships in the Early Years
Conversations to Empower Children, Professionals, Families and Communities
Sonia Mainstone-Cotton and Jamel Carly Campbell

Developing Child-Centred Practice for Safeguarding and Child Protection
Strategies for Every Early Years Setting
Rachel Buckler

Little Brains Matter
A Practical Guide to Brain Development and Neuroscience in Early Childhood
Debbie Garvey

Creativity and Wellbeing in the Early Years
Practical Ideas and Activities for Young Children
Sonia Mainstone-Cotton

Anti-Racist Practice in the Early Years
A Holistic Framework for the Wellbeing of All Children
Valerie Daniel

Speech, Language and Communication for Healthy Little Minds
Practical Ideas to Promote Communication for Wellbeing in the Early Years
Becky Poulter Jewson and Rebeca Skinner

Promoting Physical Development and Activity in Early Childhood
Practical Ideas for Early Years Settings
Jackie Musgrave, Jane Dorrian, Joanne Josephidou, Ben Langdown and Lucy Rodriguez Leon

Promoting Physical Development and Activity in Early Childhood

Practical Ideas for Early Years Settings

Jackie Musgrave, Jane Dorrian,
Joanne Josephidou, Ben Langdown
and Lucy Rodriguez Leon

Routledge
Taylor & Francis Group

LONDON AND NEW YORK

Designed cover image: Lottie is 4 years old and loves to roleplay schools and cafes, model with playdough, dance, climb, jump, splash in muddy puddles and play with her older brother Charlie and sister Lilly. This painting is of Lottie and her daddy playing tennis in the sun amongst the flowers.

First published 2024
by Routledge
4 Park Square, Milton Park, Abingdon, Oxon OX14 4RN

and by Routledge
605 Third Avenue, New York, NY 10158

Routledge is an imprint of the Taylor & Francis Group, an informa business

© 2024 Jackie Musgrave, Jane Dorrian, Joanne Josephidou, Ben Langdown and Lucy Rodriguez Leon

The right of Jackie Musgrave, Jane Dorrian, Joanne Josephidou, Ben Langdown and Lucy Rodriguez Leon to be identified as authors of this work has been asserted in accordance with sections 77 and 78 of the Copyright, Designs and Patents Act 1988.

British Library Cataloguing-in-Publication Data
A catalogue record for this book is available from the British Library

Library of Congress Cataloging-in-Publication Data
A catalog record has been requested for this book

ISBN: 978-1-032-47956-9 (hbk)
ISBN: 978-1-032-47954-5 (pbk)
ISBN: 978-1-003-38672-8 (ebk)

DOI: 10.4324/9781003386728

Typeset in Optima
by Deanta Global Publishing Services, Chennai, India

To access the free online resources accompanying this book please visit
https://resourcecentre.routledge.com/speechmark

Contents

Series Advisor foreword

This latest addition to the Little Minds Matter series delves into promoting physical development and activity in the early years. The book is slightly unique for the series, as it is written by a team of five experts offering diverse perspectives and valuable insights.

At a time where children's physical activity is below ideal levels, exacerbated by the pandemic, this book becomes an essential resource. It provides a solid foundation for understanding children's physical development and practical strategies to boost their activity.

The book covers a wide spectrum of physical development, offering guidance on increasing children's physical activity and helpful sections on sleep, growth, observing physical development, and age-specific activity recommendations. I will be sharing these with the staff and parents I work with.

Accessible and free from jargon, this book is also a valuable resource for staff teams, offering opportunities for professional development and easy-to-share information with parents and carers.

Sonia Mainstone-Cotton
Series Advisor
October 2023

Foreword

Firstly, I would like to thank you for being interested in this book. Children are precious and as the guardians of our children, whether you work in a professional context or as a parent or carer, you do one of the most important jobs there is!

Many adults often think that teaching starts when a child enters formal education; this isn't right! Babies begin to learn while still in the womb, and there is a great deal that parents and practitioners can do to promote physical activity and development right from the start. Whilst formal education is extremely important for a child to develop academic skills, children who are not ready for formal learning fall behind. One of the roles of early years practitioners is to ensure our children explore and experience a wide range of stimulating situations in a safe and positive environment; this gives children the confidence to explore new things, thus allowing them to grow and develop. All children need to be school ready, and that preparation starts with the children's family and practitioners as important people in a child's life.

This book is not just for the early years workforce, it's for everyone and anyone who is interested in helping babies and children to develop effectively, from parents to grandparents, to nursery staff and child minders – if you look after a preschool child, this book is written for you! Stimulating learning environments do not need expensive toys and equipment. It doesn't matter if you have loads of money or no money, the resources that you have in your own space are enough to enable children to explore, develop and play. Pots and pans from the kitchen, going to communal play areas and enabling your child to explore under the bedclothes are examples of everyday occurrences that can help develop physical development and promote activity.

Both this book and the online course we have created, *Supporting Physical Development in Early Childhood* (available at https://www.open.edu/openlearn/health-sports-psychology/supporting-physical-development-early-childhood), is the output from a long journey of ensuring that early years staff have access to high quality resources that enable them to support children with their physical development. Hopefully, the book will give you ideas of how to develop your understanding that the things which you do intuitively are not about keeping the children busy, but about allowing them to work out how to interact with their environment, whether it be exploring mud at the bottom of the garden or working out how to play with their peers in a way that helps them to develop. This development is essential and cannot be replaced, so it's really important to get it right.

Finally, I would like to thank Dr Lala Manners, from Active Matters, who started this journey with me, one cold wet day in London when we were in a conference! Lala made the connection with Jackie Musgrave and other colleagues at The Open University, and we worked together to turn our dream of having a high-quality course about physical activity and development into reality. Thank you one and all, great colleagues with a passion for getting it right!

Angela Baker
RGN, RSCN, BA (hons) Specialist Community Practice, MsC Public Health, UKPHR 0263, FFPH.

Introduction

Getting young children active and supporting their physical development right from the start is essential for not only children's all-round development and good health, but also for better health and wellbeing across the lifespan. The four Chief Medical Officers of the UK published their Physical Activity Guidelines in 2019, and in the introduction, they state that:

> If physical activity were a drug, we would refer to it as a miracle cure, due to the great many illnesses it can prevent and help treat.
>
> (p. 3)

However, children's levels of physical activity are not as high as they need to be, a situation that has been made worse by the restrictions caused by the pandemic. In addition, children's levels of physical development are a concern, a situation that was made worse by the restrictions imposed to limit the spread of Covid.

This book will help practitioners in pre-school education and care settings increase their knowledge and understanding about the importance of physical development and physical activity to support young children's overall development, health and wellbeing. The content highlights the benefits of promoting physical activity to children's holistic health and development. It illustrates how physical activity can improve mental health and wellbeing, as well as contributing to the prevention of childhood obesity.

The content will help adults involved in caring for and educating babies and young children to identify ways to meet the 180 minutes of physical activity that is recommended per day for all children (CMO, 2019) The approaches used to encourage physical activity will be low cost and learners will be encouraged to use the resources available to them.

The content draws on materials developed for a highly successful online free course that was produced by the book authors. The course was funded by Health Education England in partnership with Public Health England. The course has had 11,000 learners enrol since its launch in July 2020. It was the finalist in the Health and Wellbeing category of the Nursery World awards in September 2021.

Reference

CMO (2019) *UK Chief Medical Officers' Physical Activity Guidelines.* Available at https://assets.publishing.service.gov.uk/government/uploads/system/uploads/attachment_data/file/832868/uk-chief-medical-officers-physical-activity-guidelines.pdf (Accessed 25 August 2023.)

Chapter overview

There are seven chapters in this book.

Chapter 1: What is growth and development?

We tend to take young children's growth and physical development for granted meaning that, given a supportive environment, good food, enough sleep and appropriate opportunities to be physically active, it will 'just happen anyway'. In many ways this is true: they visibly grow taller and weigh more over time; baby or 'milk' teeth fall out and permanent teeth appear; hair and nails grow and need cutting; clothes and shoes require continual replacement; and they become physically more confident, competent, creative and adaptive.

But the world children now inhabit has changed significantly in the last forty years. Spaces to play freely are often limited, curricular demands affect the time available for children to be active, the increase in child obesity rates remains a serious issue, and the use of 'screentime' impacts on their motivation and level of engagement with all things physical. In short, many children are not moving enough to properly support their overall health and wellbeing and ensure smooth growth and physical development. Physical growth, development and health are inextricably linked, and this is discussed in detail within the chapter.

Chapter 2: Body systems, senses and physical development

As children physically grow and develop, their body senses and systems are also undergoing a rapid transformation. In this chapter, you will build on the knowledge gained in Chapter 1, exploring the critical importance of senses and systems and how their smooth overall development is intricately linked to movement skills and physical activity.

Chapter 3: Supporting physical development in children: The current state of babies' and children's physical development and activity

This chapter introduces readers to developing and supporting young children's movement skills. The content defines fine and gross motor skills, explaining why they are important and outlines how the skills can be supported in early childhood settings. The content explains how they link to learning and holistic development, including children's learning. It explores some of the barriers that can compromise their acquisition/rehearsal/refinement. The importance of the environment is explored, making links to Chapter 2.

Chapter 4: Movement and learning

Every time a child moves something is being learned about their bodies and how they work: about their physical relationship to each other and the environment; about concepts such as speed, distance, forces, friction, height, depth, weight, angles, direction; about mathematical ideas including space, shape, pattern; and about how non-verbal communication is used to effect positive outcomes.

The chapter looks at how adults can properly support children's learning through movement. It also looks at how we can create the optimum environments that extend children's level of physical activity.

Chapter 5: Play and physical development in early childhood

The content of this chapter explores the role of different types of play in children's physical development. It will help you to understand how to promote children's physical development through your knowledge of developmentally 'informed' practice. The content will help you to apply your understanding to plan an enabling environment which supports young children's physical development without expensive equipment or classes.

Chapter 6: Health and physical development

As around 20 per cent of children have an additional need, such as a health condition, a special educational need or mobility difficulties, it is important that such needs are examined to find ways to support physical development as well as making physical activity as inclusive as possible. This chapter explores how conditions such as asthma, sickle cell disease and diabetes can be a barrier to full participation, but importantly, it includes knowledge about steps that can be taken to overcome such barriers.

Chapter 7: Putting it into practice

The concluding chapter continues the theme of how practitioners can put what they have learned into practice. It includes a section summarising best practice in relation to working with parents. The chapter includes an audit that readers can use to assess how well their setting promotes physical activity and supports physical development. It includes case studies from different perspectives, including babies and children from 0–5.

We hope you enjoy reading our book.

Acknowledgements

Our thanks to Health Education England for funding the production of the course Supporting Physical Development in Early Childhood.

We are grateful to Angela Baker and to Dr Lala Manners for their authoring on the course.

What is growth and development?

Jane Dorrian

Introduction

Babies are moving and wriggling around before they are born; being active is hardwired into them and encouraging that desire to move is something that we should all be doing. We tend to take young children's growth and physical development for granted, assuming that if they are given a supportive environment, good food, enough sleep and appropriate opportunities to be physically active, growth and development will 'just happen'. In some ways this is true – children grow taller and weigh more over time, their baby teeth fall out and permanent teeth appear, hair and nails grow and need cutting, clothes and shoes require continual replacement and they become physically more confident and able. However, there are lots of factors that impact upon these processes. Physical growth and development are inextricably linked, but they are not the same and this chapter will look at the differences between them, how they happen and what we can do to help children's healthy growth and development.

Growing and developing

If we stop for a minute and consider more deeply, we can see that growth and development are indeed different. For example, we would say that our hair and nails grow but we wouldn't say they develop, and we might think that a child's ability to walk is developing but wouldn't say it was growing. So, what is the difference?

DOI: 10.4324/9781003386728-1

ACTIVITY

Consider this situation:

Gab is 3 years old and has been attending nursery for eight weeks. On their first day they ran over to the climbing frame and tried to climb up. They could get one foot onto the first bar and one hand onto the bar above but couldn't get the other hand or foot onto the bars. They have tried to climb to the top of the climbing frame every day, and today they did it. Do you think this is because they have grown taller and stronger or because they have developed new physical skills?

The answer is probably a combination of the two; over the course of eight weeks Gab will have grown taller and their muscles will have grown larger and stronger, but they will also have developed new skills like hand–eye co-ordination, gripping, grasping, pulling and balancing. As well as these physical skills, they will have watched other children climbing and copied their actions, which shows their cognitive, problem-solving abilities developing. They might have had support from practitioners to develop their confidence which is part of social development.

If they had just become taller, they wouldn't have been able to reach the top without developing new skills and if they had only developed the skills, they might not have got there without being taller and stronger – so we can see that growth and development are different, but they are closely connected.

Figure 1.1 Developing the skills to climb a frame requires a range of skills
Source: Stock image: Playground Climbing Frame, Pixabay

Physical growth is change that happens to the body over time. Children's size and shape change as they get older and are easy to measure; for example, lots of houses will have a doorframe with children's heights at different ages marked on it. The body grows more rapidly in the first six months after birth than at any other time. Healthy new-borns will double their birthweight by the time they are four to five months old and triple it by their first birth-day. They become taller and heavier as their bones, muscles and organs mature and these changes will happen regardless of the experiences the child has or the environment they are in, unless they are affected by specific health conditions or extreme circumstances such as neglect.

Physical growth happens in two distinct ways – from top to bottom – starting at the head and spreading down to the toes (the scientific term for this is cephalocaudal development), and from the central core out towards the fingers and toes (called proximodistal development) (Hermanussen, 2016). These patterns of growth explain why babies can control their heads before they can control their arms and legs, and why fiddly movements like tying laces or manoeuvring a pencil take a long time to achieve. To achieve these skills the bones and muscles in the hands and fingers need to be fully grown, but this doesn't happen until the child is around 4 or 5 years old, so they are not able to make the movements needed to tie the laces or control the pencil until then (Johnston and Halocha, 2010). Although the directions of growth are the same for all children, the time they take to happen is indi-vidual to each child, which is why a group of children who are the same age will not be the same height or size.

Physical development is the way in which children gain control over their bodies and the movements they make as they grow (Johnston and Nahmad-Williams, 2009). Some of these changes will happen naturally as part of maturation and developments in the brain and but others depend on the environment and experiences that the baby or child has. For exam-ple, if you place your finger into the hand of a baby, it will grasp it in a reflex action. As the baby's cognitive understanding develops, they will learn that they can choose to grasp something they want, like a toy, so will develop control over their reflex movements, and this process contin-ues as they get older. Genetics plays a part, most obviously in inherited conditions that impact on physical development such as muscular dys-trophy, but also in more general ways such as how tall a child will be or what body shape they will have, and in Chapter 6 you will explore this in greater detail. Physical development doesn't happen smoothly; it is usually 'spikey' – meaning that skills will not develop at the same time or in the same order and they happen at different speeds. You will find out more about this in Chapter 3.

CASE STUDY

Early Years Wales Active Baby at Home Programme

It is important to remember that we need to support children's physical development right from birth; just because very young babies do not appear to move very much it can be easy to assume they cannot do things, but the first 1000 days of a child's life are critical in laying the foundations for healthy holistic development and wellbeing. There are lots of projects that focus on helping new parents to introduce activities to support their baby's physical development; one of these is the Early Years Wales 'Active Baby at Home' programme.

In the sessions, parents learn about the importance of giving babies 'tummy time', where they can stretch and wriggle, explore the range of skills that need to be developed before a baby can crawl and look at the importance of providing lots of different indoor and outdoor experiences without any stress or pressure to perform or reach any expected milestone. To find out more about the programme search online for Early Years Wales Active Baby at Home.

The spikey progress that happens when children are developing one physical skill is also apparent across the range of different physical skills and all areas of holistic development. Children may not be able to describe their emotions or to explain their understanding of a situation, which shows a difference in the development of their language, emotional and cognitive skills and shows how development can link to wellbeing. Often a child's skill development will stall, and they don't seem to be making any progress (this is sometimes called plateauing) or their development can appear to go backwards, and they become unable to do things that they could do previously (this is called regression and is especially apparent during times of more rapid growth). This is a normal part of holistic development, and we need to make sure that we give children time to practice, think, watch others and be confident and comfortable about what they can do before moving onto the next level of a new skill.

CASE STUDY

Sam, Naz and Ash play together regularly; they are each 20 months old and their parents have been friends since before the children were born. Today they are playing in the local toddler group where there is a range of different apparatus suitable for small children. The children head towards a slide that is approximately one metre high and has steps up to the top made from wooden planks. There are handrails either side of the planks.

Sam can climb the steps alone, holding onto the handrails and putting both feet onto the plank before stepping up to the next one. Naz can walk up the steps confidently without using the handrails and can step up the planks from one foot to the other. Ash was a late walker and they need dad's help to keep their balance when going up the steps and keep hold of dad's hand when sliding down.

Questions

What does this case study tell us about the children's physical development?

What reasons can you think of for the differences in their development?

What other information might help you get a better understanding of their development?

Discussion

Although the children are the same age, their gross motor skills are very different. However, this range is within the norms of physical development at this age as between the ages of 0 and 2 the rate of development is at it fastest, so some children can appear to be much more advanced. This means that we need to be very careful about labelling children who are not progressing as quickly and being unable or as having a problem. In this case study, the difference between Naz and Ash appears to be big, but if we look at the difference between Naz and Sam or Sam and Ash, it is less noticeable.

In this discussion we have only looked at the children's gross motor skills; we don't know what their fine motor control is like, and we don't know about any other areas of development such as their language and communication skills, or their social and emotional development. We also don't know about the children's prior developmental experiences; for example, Ash may have been able to move around very effectively by shuffling along on their bottom and so did not have a need to start walking. We don't know if any of the children have disabilities or additional needs; for example, Sam might have a visual impairment and wear glasses which means they need to move more slowly. It is not clear whether the children are boys or girls, or whereabouts in the world the play is happening, and these are factors that can impact on rates of development too; for example, in some cultures boys are encouraged to play more physically than girls (Moyles, 2012).

When we are looking at a child's physical development, we need to make sure we gather as much information as possible and build up a full picture.

It is also important to remember that whilst children are developing physically, they are also developing in lots of other areas, for example, socially, emotionally, cognitively and all of these areas will also have an impact on their wellbeing. The areas of development are connected, and progress may often pop up in unexpected developmental areas. Children will be experimenting with different movements when they try new activities. They will discuss and trial these with their friends, identifying what they are good at, what their friends are good at, and they will apply this knowledge to new social situations and learn from each other. Children may make new friendships with others who share the same level of skill and interest. They may start to use the language of movement in different contexts, such as when they are dancing or role playing, and they will make connections between movements and shapes they have seen or heard about in pictures, poems, stories, sculptures, films and TV programmes.

Becoming more confident and competent movers and exploring and experimenting with their new physical skills can also lead to adventures which require children to become aware of risks and how to manage these, you find out more about this in Chapter 3.

Measuring growth and development

In many countries the development of a child's physical skills is monitored by a range of professionals. Parents in the UK will be familiar with the personal child health record, often called the 'red book', that health visitors complete when they undertake their regular checks on babies and toddlers (NHS, 2020).

Figure 1.2 The Red Book used by health visitors in the UK

These checks include measuring the child's height and weight, which are recorded on charts that monitor growth and can be used to check that the child is making progress (MacBlain et al., 2017). When children start nursery or school, they will often undergo a 'baseline assessment' that measures their skills across a range of developmental areas. The information on these charts and assessments is based on developmental norms which indicate how an average child would grow and develop (Dorrian, 2022).

Developmental norms are used to monitor many aspects of a child's development and they are often identified when a child reaches a 'milestone', an observable or measurable skill such as being able to sit up or being able to take five steps. To achieve some of the milestones a child will need to have gained specific physical development skills, such as being able to make large movements with their arms and legs (known as gross motor skills) and to control small movements with their toes and fingers (fine motor skills), and you will explore these in greater detail in Chapter 3. Milestones are usually linked to an approximate age by which a child should be able to demonstrate the skill: for example, most children start walking at between 13 and 15 months. There are norms and milestones covering all areas of a child's development and they are used by practitioners working in health, education and social care to help them monitor and support children's progress (NHS Greater Glasgow and Clyde, n.d.).

Although we are focusing on children's physical development here, it is important to remember that all areas of a child's development are connected and are happening at the same time because lots of activities depend on different skills working together. For example, you might see a baby use their fingers to grasp a piece of banana in their hand (a physical skill), move their arm to bring it to their mouth to explore the taste and texture (a sensory skill) and then smile to show their enjoyment (a social skill). Many of the physical skills that we try to support and develop when we are working with babies and young children are made up of lots of other skills that are learned over a period of time. For example, before a child can use a pencil correctly, they must be able to manipulate large objects like blocks and balls and once they have mastered that they can progress to more complex, finer skills like finger painting and threading beads. It is only after they can complete those movements that they will be able to grasp and guide a pencil to make a mark. Alongside these physical elements, they need to have an understanding of the role of mark-making and a desire to want to do that, which is linked to cognitive development. Providing developmentally appropriate opportunities for children to progress thorough these skills journeys and supporting them at each stage impacts positively on their wellbeing, allows them to succeed and builds their confidence, which makes them more likely to experiment and try new things (Colwell, 2015).

TIME TO REFLECT

Think about a time that you have learnt a new physical skill – it could be playing a computer game, knitting, dancing, yoga. How did you feel when you began to do it? How did you feel when it 'clicked'? Did you use any techniques to help you perfect it, like talking to yourself, or writing notes? What impact did the process have on your wellbeing? How did you describe the process when talking about it with friends?

Your reflection shows that physical development doesn't happen in isolation; we experience emotions, use language and apply our thinking skills as part of the process.

Norms and milestones can be really useful for practitioners because they give us a general idea about what the next step in a child's development might be and help us make sure we are providing suitable activities to support their progress, but we need to remember that there is no such thing as typical child. As we mentioned earlier in the chapter, children of the same age will be different sizes and their skills will be developing in a way that is unique to them. There are also lots of other factors that can affect the norms such as additional learning needs, disabilities and cultural factors. Children's moods and wellbeing levels alter from day to day and hour to hour in the same way that ours do, so we do need to be mindful of recognising these issues. Pushing a child to perform a skill before they are developmentally ready can affect their wellbeing, making them feel anxious and denting their confidence and self-worth (Glazzard et al., 2019).

Healthy bodies

At the start of this chapter, we looked at the differences between growth and physical development and learned that growth is a maturation process that involves changes to the size and shape of a child's body. Although to a certain extent these changes will happen regardless of the environment a child is in, there are a range of factors that have a positive impact on a child's growth. These are explored in the following sections.

Sleep

When children sleep, a growth hormone called somatotropin is released into their system, so a lack of sleep will affect their growth rate (Abbott and Burkitt, 2023). Not getting enough sleep can also affect the production of other hormones and has been shown to increase the likelihood of a child becoming overweight or obese, with some studies suggesting that the children who have the lowest amounts of sleep are 76% more likely to be overweight compared to those who have the recommended amount (Fry and Rehman, 2022; Ruan et al., 2015). Table 1.1 below shows the recommended amount of time a child should be sleeping according to their age.

When children are asleep, they often wriggle around, stretch out and even fall out of bed and the movements that they make help to build muscle strength and improve their mobility, so having enough quality sleep is really important (Birch et al., 2011).

Getting children to go to sleep can be a challenge. Getting into a routine before bedtime is a good way to help create good sleep habits. One important factor that affects everyone's ability to get to sleep is blue light. This light is present in natural daylight, and it triggers the production of hormones that control our body's internal clock, so when the light fades our bodies know it's time to sleep. Blue light is also emitted by electronic devices like phones, televisions, and tablets and this can confuse our body clocks into thinking that it is not time to sleep (Brockmann, 2016). So, part of a good sleep routine should involve getting children outside in the natural light every day and making sure that they are not using screens for at least two hours before bedtime (Great Ormond Street Hospital, 2020). This helps to ensure their hormone levels are balanced and they will get the high-quality sleep that supports growth.

Table 1.1 Recommended sleep times

Child's age	Recommended amount of sleep time in 24 hours
4–12 months	12 to 16 hours including naps
1–2 years	11 to 14 hours including naps
3–5 years	10 to 13 hours including naps
6–12 years	9 to 12 hours

(World Health Organisation (WHO), 2019)

Physical activity

Getting active and moving increases the blood flow around the body and this helps to ensure that the different systems within the body grow healthily (WHO, 2022). One of the systems that benefits is the immune system because the increases in heart rate and blood flow, plus the production of hormones such as adrenaline that happen when children get active, trigger their immune cells to 'patrol' the body and target viruses and bacteria that could cause illness and affect growth (Wadley et al. 2020). Muscles, tendons and ligaments also need good blood supplies to grow healthily and performing lots of different types of activity and movements helps to develop bone strength.

To make sure that children have as many opportunities as possible to get active, they need to be able to play inside and outside, because these different spaces allow children to play in a variety of ways. Outdoor spaces help children to perform the big gross motor movements like jumping, rolling and climbing, which support the development of strong bones and can be difficult to do safely in confined spaces indoors. Being outdoors also exposes children to natural sunlight, which helps develop good sleep patterns (Harrison, 2004), as well as helping the body to produce vitamin D (from exposure to sunlight), which is important in the growth of healthy bones. Our bodies need vitamin D to transfer calcium from food and drink into the bones, so even if a child is getting a healthy diet, they need to spend time being active outside to make sure they get maximum benefits.

Nutrition

Babies and young children need a well-balanced diet that provides them with all the nutrients required for healthy growth. The nutritional needs of babies and young children are not the same as those of adults; up until the age of around six months all a baby's nutrition will come from breast milk or formula and then they need to be introduced to a range of different types of food (NHS, 2022). Encouraging children to eat as wide a variety of food as possible is vital because poor diets that provide too much or too little of a particular food group can result in malnutrition and children who are affected by this in the first four years of their lives tend not to catch up with normal growth patterns throughout their lives (UNICEF, 2019).

TIME TO REFLECT

By the time they are 5, a child should be eating a well-balanced diet that includes a range of different food groups, but around the world, issues related to nutrition are complex and as our communities become more diverse, we need to recognise these. Take a look at the two images on the following pages: one shows the daily food requirements recommended in the UK and the other shows the recommendations in Japan. What similarities and differences can you see between them?

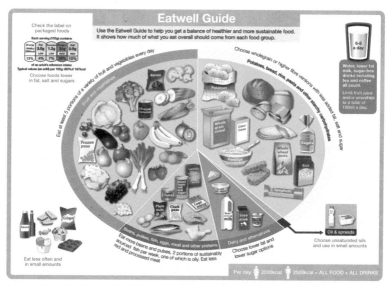

Figure 1.3 The Eatwell plate
Source: Public Health England. https://assets.publishing.service.gov.uk/media/5a75564fed915d6faf2b2375/Eatwell_guide_colour.pdf

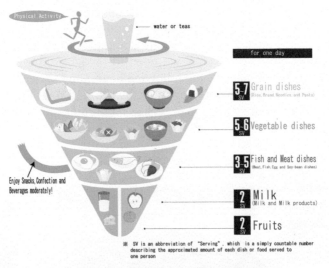

Japanese Food Guide Spinning Top
Do you have a well-balanced diet?

Physical Activity

water or teas

for one day

5-7 SV Grain dishes (Rice, Bread, Noodles, and Pasta)

5-6 SV Vegetable dishes

3-5 SV Fish and Meat dishes (Meat, Fish, Egg and Soy-bean dishes)

2 SV Milk (Milk and Milk products)

2 SV Fruits

Enjoy Snacks, Confection and Beverages moderately!

※ SV is an abbreviation of "Serving", which is a simply countable number describing the approximated amount of each dish or food served to one person

Decided by Ministry of Health, Labour and Welfare and Ministry of Agriculture, Forestry and Fisheries.

Figure 1.4 The Japanese Food Guide Spinning Top
Source: https://www.mhlw.go.jp/bunya/kenkou/pdf/eiyou-syokuji5.pdf

Discussion

You will see that the same food groups are identified but the Japanese recommendations separate fruits and vegetables, and do not list oils and spreads. The order that the foods are listed under the headings is also important; the Japanese recommendations put fish before meat and rice before bread. This is because different cultures have different 'staple' foods. For example, potatoes are a staple in many north European diets, but around the world this could be yam, millet or sorghum, which are foods we might not be familiar with in the UK. This shows us that the contents of a balanced diet will not be the same for every community, but getting the range of different food groups is the important point.

Whilst sleep, physical activity and nutrition promote growth, they also support healthy development, and there are other factors that support this too.

Environment

Children need lots of different places and spaces where they can practice and refine their gross and fine motor skills safely to suit each context. They need to be able to move around the spaces and explore by themselves to help them develop independence, make mistakes and get into situations that they need to solve, which will also help them to develop cognitively, socially and emotionally. They need to be given opportunities to explore the environments by trying out different ways of moving and being active and taking risks, which also helps them to develop strategies that impact positively on their wellbeing.

Children do not need specialist resources either; an empty box can provide opportunities for endless activities. The picture below shows how a child used an empty box and some strips of paper and fabric to make a den which they used as a cave, a bedroom, a classroom and many other things!

Figure 1.5 Using everyday items to make a den

As well as being inside and outdoors, children need times and places to be alone and rest, to play with other children, to use apparatus and resources, to be in empty spaces and as many other options as possible. There are lots of sport-based activities that are promoted for young children, and these can provide useful development opportunities, but we need to remember that physical activity is a lot more than just organised sports (Fraser-Thomas and Safai, 2018).

Providing a range of enjoyable daily opportunities for children to move freely from birth onwards plays a vital role in supporting their smooth growth and overall development. Making changes that seem small, like encouraging children to play barefoot, can make big differences:

> Barefoot walking helps children develop balance, proprioception, and body awareness- children who spend more time barefoot have better control when they are running, climbing, and playing.
>
> (Watkins, 2022, p. 68)

Positive adult support

If children see the adults around them enjoying being active and moving around, they are much more likely to have a positive emotional response and enjoy it too. As adults, we need to provide positive support to help children make progress and make the mistakes that allow them to learn and perfect the skills they have developed and progress onto the next steps.

TIME TO REFLECT

Sometimes we intervene and limit a child's opportunity to practise their physical skills; for example, if they have spilled sand on the floor, we might step in to clean it up quickly so that other children don't slip on it rather than supporting the child to use the dustpan and brush and learn how to sweep up. Can you think of a time you have done something like this? Why did you react that way and could you have responded differently?

Obstacles to healthy growth and physical development

The world children live in now has changed significantly in the last 40 years. Spaces to play freely are often limited, curricular demands affect the time available for children to be active, the increase in childhood obesity rates remains a serious issue, and the use of 'screentime' impacts on their motivation and level of engagement with all things physical (Duncombe and Preedy, 2021; Waite, 2017; Sajaniemi, 2017). The COVID-19 pandemic made it even more difficult to provide opportunities for children to get physically active. In short, many children are not moving enough to properly support their overall health and wellbeing and ensure smooth growth and physical development.

We have already discussed some of the factors that can affect healthy physical growth and development, such as nutrition, sleep and access to a safe environment. Figure 1.6 shows a range of other issues that can have a negative impact that will be explored in later chapters.

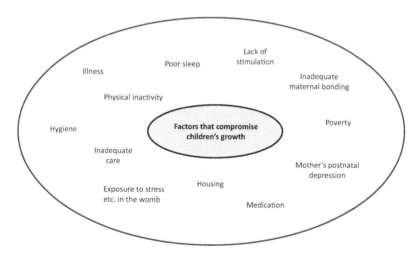

Figure 1.6 Factors that compromise children's growth

Discussion

All these factors are closely connected; for example, living in poverty is likely to result in poor housing which is more likely to be damp or mouldy and this increases the likelihood of illnesses such as asthma (Nelson, 2014). As practitioners, there is a limit to the direct impact we can make on some of these complex social issues, but there are areas that we can help to raise parents' and carers' awareness to support their child's physical development and growth.

ACTIVITY

Read the information below about 'containers'.

If you look around any baby and child shop you will see lots of different equipment designed to 'contain' children and keep them in one place, things like highchairs, rockers and pushchairs. Whilst all of these are useful to help us support children in particular situations such as feeding times, they are increasingly being used to 'hold' children whilst adults are doing other things, for example putting the child in the highchair whilst we tidy up. Spending too long sitting in containers stops children making the essential spontaneous movements like wriggling, stretching and bouncing that help strengthen all the muscles that support the spine. Having strong muscles is vital in making sure that a child's hips and shoulders are in the right position to start crawling and walking, so having lots of time to move freely throughout the day helps them prepare for this (Marlen, 2019).

How could you use this information to help parents and carers support their child's physical growth and development?

You might want to consider:

- Points in day that lend themselves to encouraging movement, like after a nap or before a bath.
- Places that can used to encourage different types of movement, like outdoor spaces.

- Ways to include children in the activities that the adults are doing so that they do not need to be placed in 'containers' for so long.

Talk to your friends, colleagues and family members and discuss how the factors that support and compromise children's physical development may be present in your environment and what you could do to minimise the obstacles to healthy growth and physical development.

Supporting growth and development in practice

There are plenty of debates about the role of early childhood in getting children 'ready for school' and the extent to which we should be focusing on this or not. Regardless of your opinion, we need to be aware that a child's ability to make any transition in their life is very dependent on their level of physical skills, and the move into preschool, nursery or reception is no exception. For them to be able to navigate the school day with ease and enjoyment they need a range of prior movement experiences. As well as the gross motor skills needed to move around and fine motor skills needed to perform tasks such as writing, there are other physical skills that we can sometimes forget or take for granted, like being able to sit still. This is one of the hardest things for young children to do because it needs high levels of balance and control which 'can only be developed by lots of movement' (O'Connor and Daly, 2016, p. 152) and is another aspect that can be affected by the overuse of 'containers', yet many teachers and practitioners expect children to be able to do it as soon as they arrive in the setting. This example shows the need for practitioners and settings to be ready to help support children's development when they arrive at settings rather than expecting them to already be able do things, and also reminds us again of why we need to consider a child's development and wellbeing holistically. As we have discovered, growth or physical development do not happen in isolation; they are connected to all the areas of development that a child goes through and there are a huge range of factors and issues that impact upon them.

ACTIVITY

The circles in the Venn diagram (Figure 1.7) represent different areas of a child's holistic development.

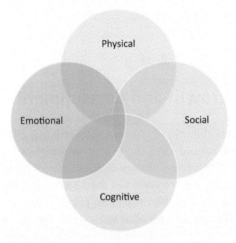

Figure 1.7 Areas of holistic development

Take a look at the activities listed below and consider where you think they best fit. Are any of them only physical development skills? Do any of them cover all four areas? Does it depend on the context?

- Dancing
- Feeding yourself
- Running in a race with friends
- Cutting out shapes
- Playing hide and seek
- Using a scooter
- Painting a picture
- Completing a jigsaw
- Spinning around to get dizzy

Think about the activities that are available for children in your setting. Where would you place them on the diagram? Are there more in one section than the others or are all the areas balanced? Can you think of other activities you could include to make sure all areas are covered?

Concluding thoughts

The growth and physical development of every child is unique and individual. The early years of a child's life are vital in enabling children to become competent and confident movers who are able to manage their bodies with fluency and ease in a range of situations and environments. By being positive role models who are active and move around, providing environments and opportunities for children to explore movement and develop their control, skills and wellbeing, we are giving them the best possible start in life.

Top tips

- Everyday items like boxes, newspapers and empty plastic bottles can be used as resources to support children's physical development so don't throw them away.
- Remember that sleep and nutrition are just as important as movement in supporting a child's physical development.
- Give children time to experiment, explore and make mistakes so that they can learn and perfect their skills.

Key terms

| Holistic development | All the interconnected aspects of a child's development, including cognitive, social, emotional and physical |
| Genetic | Physical and biological aspects inherited from parents |

Maturation	The process which governs the rate at which physical growth and development happen
Milestones	The achievement of observable or measurable skills
Norms	Recognised standards or measures of progress based on a sample of the population
Physical development	The process of growing, changing and developing control over the body
Physical growth	The processes by which the body increases in size
Plateauing	When the development of a particular skill stops progressing for a period of time
Regression	When a child cannot perform a skill with the same level of competence that they previously could
Motor skill	The control and movement of specific muscles to perform a task

In the next chapter, we explore the importance of the body's systems and senses, and how these are intricately linked to children's wellbeing, holistic development, and good physical and mental health.

 Further reading

Connell, G. and McCarthy, C. (2014) *A Moving Child is a Learning Child: How the Body Teaches the Brain to Think*, Minneapolis, MN: Free Spirit Publishing.

Manners, L. (2019) *The Early Years Movement Handbook: A Principles-Based Approach to Supporting Young Children's Physical Development, Health and Wellbeing*, London: Jessica Kingsley Publishers.

References

Abbott, R. And Burkitt, E. (2023) *Child Development and the Brain: From Embryo to Adolescence*. Bristol: Policy Press.

Birch, L.L., Burns, A.C. and Parker, L. (2011) *Early Childhood Obesity Prevention Policies*. Washington, DC: National Academies Press.

Brockmann, P.E., Diaz, B., Damiani, F., Villarroel, L., Núñez, F. and Bruni, O. (2016) 'Impact of television on the quality of sleep in preschool children', *Sleep Medicine*, 20, pp. 140–144. Available at: https://www.sciencedirect.com/science/article/abs/pii/S1389945715008229 (Accessed 31st May 2023.)

Colwell, J. (2015) *Reflective Teaching in Early Education*. London: Bloomsbury.

Dorrian, J. (2022) 'Rethinking the design of school readiness assessments', in Betts, A. and Thai K. P. (eds) *Handbook of Research on Innovative Approaches to Early Childhood Development and School Readiness*. New York: IGI Global, pp. 96–112.

Duncombe, R. and Preedy, P. (2021) 'Physical development in the early years: Exploring its importance and the adequacy of current provision in the United Kingdom', *Education 3–13*, 49(8), pp. 920–934.

Fraser-Thomas, J. and Safai, P. (2018) 'Tykes and 'Timbits': A critical examination of organised sport for prechoolers'. In Dionigi R.A. and Gard, M. (eds) *Sport & Physical Activity Across the Lifespan*. London: Palgrave Macmillan, pp. 93–116.

Fry, A. and Rehman, A. (2022) *Obesity and Sleep*. Available at: https://www.sleepfoundation.org/physical-health/obesity-and-sleep#references-78805 (Accessed 1st June 2023.)

Glazzard, J., Potter, M. and Stones, S. (2019) *Meeting the Mental Health Needs of Young Children*. St Albans: Critical Publishing.

Great Ormond Street Hospital (2020) *Sleep Hygiene in Children and Young People*. Available at: https://www.gosh.nhs.uk/conditions -and-treatments/procedures-and-treatments/sleep-hygiene -children/ (Accessed 1st June 2023.)

Harrison, Y. (2004) 'The relationship between daytime exposure to light and night-time sleep in 6–12-week-old infants', *Journal of Sleep Research*, 13(4), pp. 345–352.

Hermanussen, M. (2016) 'Growth in Childhood and Puberty', in Kumanov, P. and Agarwal, A. (eds) *Puberty*. Cham, Switzerland: Springer, pp. 65–76.

Johnston, J. and Halocha, J. (2010) *Early Childhood and Primary Education Readings and Reflections*. Berkshire, UK: McGraw-Hill.

Johnston, J. and Nahmad-Williams, L. (2009) *Early Childhood Studies*. London: Pearson.

MacBlain, S., Dunn, J. and Luke, I. (2017) *Contemporary Childhood*. London: Sage.

Marlen, D. (2019) 'Natural physical development in the first year: Learning from the Pikler approach', in Duncombe, R. (ed.) *The Physical Development Needs of Young Children*. Oxford: Routledge, pp. 77–89.

Moyles, J.R. (2012) *A–Z of Play in Early Childhood*. Maidenhead: Open University Press.

Nelson, R. (2014) 'Poor housing quality linked to asthma flare ups', *The Lancet*, 2(12), p. 974.

NHS (2020) *Your Baby's Health and Development Reviews*. Available at: https://www.nhs.uk/conditions/baby/babys-development/height -weight-and-reviews/baby-reviews/ (Accessed 31st May 2023.)

NHS (2022) *Your Baby's First Solid Foods*. Available at: https://www .nhs.uk/conditions/baby/weaning-and-feeding/babys-first-solid -foods/ (Accessed 31st May 2023.)

NHS Greater Glasgow and Clyde (n.d.) *Child Development Timeline*. Available at: https://www.nhsggc.org.uk/kids/child-development/ interactive-child-development-timeline/ (Accessed 31st May 2023.)

O'Connor, A. and Daly, A. (2016) *Understanding Physical Development in the Early Years: Linking Bodies and Minds*. London: Routledge.

Public Health England (2016) *Eatwell Guide.* Available at: https://assets .publishing.service.gov.uk/government/uploads/system/uploads/ attachment_data/file/528193/Eatwell_guide_colour.pdf (Accessed 31st May 2023.)

Ruan, H., Xun, P., Cai, W., He, K. and Tang, Q. (2015) 'Habitual sleep duration and risk of childhood obesity: Systematic review and dose-response meta-analysis of prospective cohort studies', *Sci. Rep.* 5, p. 16160; doi: 10.1038/srep16160.

Sajaniemi, N. (2017) 'The stressed child', in Owen, A. (ed.) *Childhood Today.* London: Sage, pp. 74–87.

UNICEF (2019) *The State of the World's Children: Children, Food and Nutrition: Growing Well in a Changing World.* Available at: https:// www.unicef.org/media/106506/file/The%20State%20of%20the %20World%E2%80%99s%20Children%202019.pdf (Accessed 23rd November 2023.)

Wadley, A., Lucas, S. and Johnson, B. (2020) *Physical Activity, Exercise and Immune Function.* Available at: https://www.rcgp.org.uk/ getmedia/e500d126-0419-479f-b99b-217d19b1c7e9/RCGPRCN CSPBasemM2MFactsheetPAExerciseImmuneFunction0820FINAL .pdf (Accessed 1st June 2023.)

Waite, L. and Prichard. E. (2017) 'The fat child', in Owen, A. (ed.) *Childhood Today.* London: Sage, pp. 125–138.

Watkins, S. (2022) *Outdoor Play for Healthy Little Minds.* London: Routledge.

World Health Organisation (WHO) (2019) 'Guidelines on physical activity, sedentary behaviour and sleep for children under 5 years of age'. Available at: https://www.who.int/publications/i/item /9789241550536 (Accessed 1st June 2023.)

World Health Organisation (WHO) (2022) *Physical Activity.* Available at: https://www.who.int/news-room/fact-sheets/detail/physical -activity (Accessed 31st May 2023.)

Body systems, senses and physical development

Joanne Josephidou and Lucy Rodriguez Leon

Introduction

This chapter explores the importance of the body's systems and senses, and how these are intricately linked to children's wellbeing, holistic development and good physical and mental health. Human bodies are complex organs made up of many interconnected systems which work seamlessly together. When these systems are functioning well, we feel comfortable and we effortlessly do many things that we usually take for granted, such as moving, breathing, eating and sleeping.

The chapter begins by looking at body systems; however, there are too many to cover them all. Therefore, we will focus on the circulatory system, the respiratory system, the muscular-skeletal system and the nervous system. These systems are inextricably linked to physical activity; they are strengthened by exercise, which in turn enables us to engage in more complex and intense physical activity.

The second section explores the body's senses, including vision, hearing, smell, taste and touch, and two of the lesser-known senses, the vestibular sense (sense of balance) and proprioceptive sense (sense of space). The sensory systems send the brain a vast amount of information about what is happening in the environment and the body. Sensory integration is the process by which the body organises, interprets and reacts to the information it receives. Just like the body systems, the senses and sensory integration develop early in life through rich experiences, play and physical activity.

DOI: 10.4324/9781003386728-2

The final section explores the idea of 'sensory rich environments' and how your knowledge of the body systems and senses can be applied in practice. We will consider the idea of 'affordance' and reflect on how the environments and materials that children access can optimise (or constrain) their sensory experiences and physical activity.

Understanding the role of body systems

The circulatory system

The circulatory system is responsible for moving blood throughout the body; it is made up of the heart and a vast network of blood vessels. It is through this system that oxygen, nutrients and hormones are delivered to our cells, and it is also the system responsible for carrying waste products, such as carbon dioxide, away.

The heart is a muscle that pumps blood around the body. It is made up of four chambers: the left and right atria, and the left and right ventricles. The atria collect the blood and pump it to the ventricles, where it is pumped into the blood vessels. There are three types of blood vessels: arteries, veins and capillaries. Arteries carry oxygen rich blood away from the heart at high pressure; these blood vessels become smaller as they move away from the heart, until they connect to tiny capillaries that reach every part of the body. Capillaries have thin walls that enable substances to move by diffusion in and out of cells. Capillaries connect to veins, the vessels that take the blood back towards the heart. Therefore, blood flows from heart→ artery→ capillary→ vein→ heart (Pocock, Richards and Richards, 2013).

This process is called circulation; however, humans have two circulatory systems. Systemic circulation is how blood goes to most of the body. Pulmonary circulation is how blood collects oxygen from the lungs. In this double circulatory system, blood travels from the heart > lungs> heart > body > heart, in a 'figure of eight' sequence.

When a baby is in the womb, blood bypasses the lungs, as these are filled with fluid; oxygen and nutrient-rich blood are supplied to the baby via the placenta. At birth, when a baby takes their first breath, the pulmonary circulation takes over and the heart begins pumping blood to the lungs to

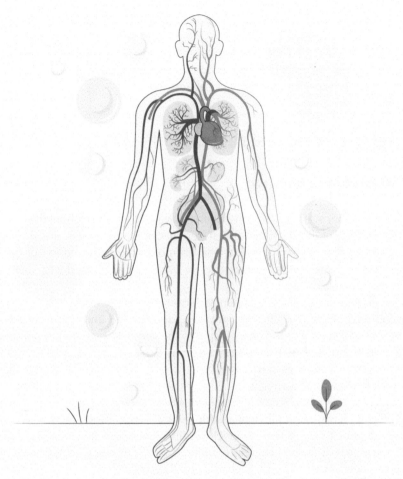

Figure 2.1 The circulatory system
Source: Image by Storyset on Freepik

collect oxygen, and then to the rest of the body. Therefore, from the moment we take our first breath, the circulatory system is interlinked with the respiratory system.

When we are physically active, the muscles have to work harder, and therefore need more oxygen. You will have noticed that your heart rate increases when you exercise. However, exercise also makes the heart muscle stronger, so that it can pump more blood with every beat. Regular exercise also increases the number of capillaries in muscles, so that blood can reach the muscles more efficiently. So, the circulatory system both enables physical activity and is strengthened by physical activity.

The respiratory system

The respiratory system is responsible for bringing oxygen into the body and expelling carbon dioxide through a complex process that starts and finishes with breathing. The respiratory system is made up of multiple organs, although it has two main parts. The upper respiratory tract includes the nose, mouth, throat and sinuses (air-filled spaces above and behind the nose). The lower respiratory tract is made up of the windpipe (trachea), airways in the lungs (bronchi, bronchioles and alveoli) and the diaphragm.

HUMAN RESPIRATORY SYSTEM

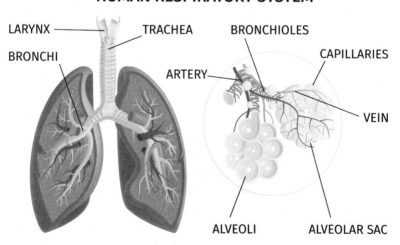

Figure 2.2 The respiratory system
Source: Image by macrovector on Freepik

Respiration begins as air is inhaled through the nose or mouth. The air then travels down the trachea and into bronchioles in the lungs, where oxygen is exchanged for carbon dioxide. The diaphragm, a dome-shaped muscle located at the bottom of the lungs, plays a crucial role in this process by contracting and expanding to help move air in and out of the lungs. The oxygenated blood is carried to the heart to be pumped through the circulatory system, where carbon dioxide is collected to return to the lungs to be exhaled (Sherwood, 2015).

Adults and older children breathe about 12–20 times per minute when resting; however, even moderate exercise, such as climbing the stairs, can cause you to breathe more rapidly to meet your body's demand for oxygen. Younger children naturally breathe more rapidly; toddlers breathe 20–30 times per minute and babies breathe 30–60 times a minute. That adds up to 17,000–30,000 breaths per day!

Just as physical activity strengthens the muscles and the heart, it also strengthens the muscles around the lungs such as the diaphragm, abdominal and intercostal muscles which enable the lungs to expand so that we can breathe more deeply and effectively.

The muscular-skeletal system

The muscular-skeletal system is a complex network of bones, joints, muscles, ligaments and tendons, that work together to provide support and enable the body to move.

In addition to enabling the body to move, bones have three other important functions. They support the body's structure, they protect vital organs and they play a part in the production of blood cells. There are 206 bones in the adult human body and over 300 bones in a baby's body, although when babies are born, some of their bones are soft like cartilage. As babies grow older, their bones begin to fuse and become more solid, until they are strong enough to enable them to start moving independently.

Bones are rigid, so the skeleton has joints to allow the body to move. Skeletal muscles are attached to bones by tendons; however, muscles can only contract and relax. This means that muscles can only pull bones; they cannot push them back and therefore, they always work in pairs (called antagonistic muscles). One muscle in the pair pulls the bone in one direction, and the other muscle pulls it back again. For example, for the lower leg to move up and down at the knee joint, the hamstring muscles and the quadricep muscles work together.

The muscular-skeletal system allows the human body to perform the smallest of movements, such as typing, to the most complex movements, such as advanced gymnastics skills. Muscles that are used frequently develop and grow strong; those that are not used fail to fully develop, or they shrink and become weak. Therefore, provision of plenty of opportunities for movement is crucial for babies and young children's growth, health and physical development.

The nervous system

The final body system we will explore in this chapter is the nervous system – a complex network of cells that transmit signals between different parts of the body. The nervous system consists of two main parts: the **central nervous system** includes the brain and spinal cord. The **peripheral nervous system** is made up mainly of nerves (bundles of long fibres called neurons) that connect to every part of the body (Sherwood, 2015).

This system is responsible for receiving information from the environment through our sensory systems, processing that information, and then sending signals to the appropriate parts of the body to produce a response. It enables the brain to sense what is going on in the body, then work in tandem with other body systems to respond and maintain equilibrium. For example, if it is hot, the brain tells the blood vessels to dilate (become wider) to reduce body temperature, if it is cold, the brain sends signals to the muscles causing us to shiver, to warm the body up. Physical activity stimulates and refines the nervous system and cause the body to respond by increasing respiration, heart rate and metabolism.

The nervous system begins to develop soon after conception. The neural tube, which eventually becomes the brain and spinal cord, forms within the first few weeks of gestation. Over the course of pregnancy, neurons continue to develop rapidly, and during the first few years of life connections between neurons are formed and are strengthened, based on the child's experiences. As the nervous system develops, babies gain control over their movements and begin to sense and respond to the world around them.

In this section we have explored four body systems that are important for understanding young children's physical development and activity. However, there are others, such as the digestive system and renal /urinary system, amongst others. The human body is complex, and whilst each body system has its own functions and role, these systems are all interconnected; they work together to keep our bodies functioning well. Understanding how our body systems work together enables us to appreciate the importance of physical activity (along with good nutrition, fresh air and sleep) for children's holistic development, health and wellbeing.

TIME TO REFLECT

- How do you talk to young children about these important body systems?
- Do you think this is important knowledge to share? Why?
- How can children learn about how their body works in age-appropriate ways?

Understanding the role of the senses

It is due to our senses that we are aware of our immediate environment and can interpret the world around us. In addition, our sensory systems also give us some information about what is going on inside our bodies. In this section we will explore seven of the body's senses, and how they integrate to provide us with information and enable us to function in our everyday lives. You will probably be familiar with the five traditional senses – sight, hearing, touch, smell and taste. However, we also have several other lesser-known senses, and two of these, vestibular sense (sense of balance) and proprioceptive sense (sense of space), are particularly important for children's physical development and physical activity.

Our different sensory systems collect information and send messages to the brain to be interpreted. For example, when we smell smoke, we know there may be a fire, or we see an obstacle in our path and avoid it. It is because of our senses that we move our hand away from a hot kettle – if it were not for our sense of touch, we would not know we were getting burnt; neither would we experience the warm silkiness of stroking a cat.

Our senses produce a large amount of information at once, and our brains must integrate and organise all this information through a process known as sensory integration. It is important that babies and children have plenty of opportunities to experience the world through all their senses, and movement is essential for sensory integration. This section will look at each of these seven senses in turn and explore why they are so important for children's holistic development and wellbeing.

Hearing

By about 28 weeks of gestation, a baby's auditory system is fully formed, and they can hear sounds such as their mother's heartbeat and digestive system, and also some sounds from outside the womb, such as voices or music. Shortly after birth, the fluid drains from the ear canals and babies begin to hear much more clearly.

As babies and young children grow and develop, they begin to differentiate between high and low frequency sounds and begin to a detect the direction a sound is coming from. With experience, they learn what different sounds mean, such as speech, a ringing phone, a door opening, or a smoke alarm. Hearing is important in the development of verbal language; babies begin to copy the sounds they hear, and when they receive a positive response from their carers, they repeat these sounds. You might have noticed that young children's babble takes on the intonation of their home language or languages. It is important for babies and young children to have their hearing tested at regular intervals during the first few years of life, so any problems are usually detected early.

Rhythmic sound tends to stimulate movement; in fact, on occasions, you may have found yourself bobbing along to the beat of a favourite tune quite subconsciously. The same is true for children; music is a great way to encourage free and expressive movement.

Vision

Many of us take our sight for granted, but human vision is a complex process. To focus on something, or to 'see', the eye detects images through light reflecting off objects, which travels onto the curved part of your eye called the retina. The retina sends messages to the brain, which interprets visual stimuli through comparison with experiences made earlier in life. In essence, babies must 'learn' to see.

The development of babies' eyes begins shortly after conception and continues until they are about 12 months old. Newborn babies do not have good vision; only objects at about 25–30 cm away are in focus, that's about the distance between a mother's breast and her face; everything else is a blur. During the first few months, babies begin to detect and understand facial expression and recognise the facial features of their parents and carers. By four months most babies begin to see things more clearly, and during the first few years of life, most children will begin to notice small details in an environment or a picture. They start to notice similarities and differences and make sense of things that are only partly visible. Babies' developing visual skills support their physical development; they begin to reach for objects they can see and learn to manoeuvre their bodies around obstacles in the environment. Sight enables children to crawl, walk, run, jump, climb, or skip freely in an environment.

Smell and taste

Smell and taste are important for children's health and wellbeing, although the significance of these senses is not always fully acknowledged. Young children have sight and hearing checks, but they don't tend to have smell and taste checks! Most newborn babies have an innate ability to recognise the smell and taste of breast milk, and babies quickly learn to recognise their mother by smell (Winberg and Porter, 1998). Smell and taste are closely linked to emotion; you may recall a time when an odour, or smell, has reminded you of something, and may have evoked powerful feelings of nostalgia, happiness, sadness and even fear.

Our sense of smell is also known as olfaction; humans can detect a vast range of different odours due to hundreds of receptors at the back of the nose. Different receptors are activated by different odour molecules; these receptors send signals to the brain to be interpreted as different smells. Humans can differentiate between about 10,000 different odours. Interestingly, research indicates that physical activity improves the identification of odour and affects the intensity with which we smell odour as we age (Cournoyer et al., 2022).

Our sense of taste is also known as gustation; the tongue has thousands of tiny taste buds that sense the taste of everything they encounter. There are five main tastes: sweet, sour, savoury, salty and bitter. Some taste buds respond to just one taste, whilst others respond to all five main tastes. This information is sent to the brain, where the taste is interpreted and builds up a sense of the overall flavour of the food.

Smell and taste are closely linked; young children soon learn to recognise foods they like and dislike, by both taste and smell. You might notice a toddler refusing to eat food before they have even tasted it; this is due to smell. It is estimated that 80–90% of what we believe we taste is actually due to smell.

Touch

The skin is the largest organ in the human body; it contains a vast system of sense receptors which detect different sorts of sensation. Some receptors detect temperature, whilst others detect pressure, pain or very light touch. When a sensory receptor is stimulated, messages are sent through the nervous system, which allows us to feel sensation in the corresponding part of the body. Touch sensation can also trigger a reflex action, enabling the body to respond subconsciously. For example, when cold receptors are triggered, little hairs on the skin stand upright to trap warm air next to the skin. Touch receptors cover the entire body, but receptors in some parts of the body are more sensitive to different sorts of touch; for example, the lips, fingertips and soles of the feet are more sensitive to light touch. Physical activity develops children's sense of touch by providing opportunities for touch receptors to be exposed to a wide range of different sensations.

Touch is the first sense babies become aware of; from birth and throughout life, it plays an important role in supporting emotional and physical wellbeing. Touch is crucial in forming secure attachment between babies and their care givers, and it builds a sense of trust and security. In fact, touch deprivation can have a detrimental effect on babies' holistic development (Field, 2010).

Vestibular sense

The vestibular sense is the first of the lesser-known senses we will discuss in this chapter. The vestibular sense is vital for physical development and activity, as it is responsible for our sense of balance. The vestibular organs are located in the inner ear, and mostly function at a subconscious level. In essence, the vestibular sense is like a gyroscope for the body, enabling us to know whether we are upright or upside down and helps us to perceive the direction and speed we are moving (Day and Fitzpatrick, 2005).

A well-developed vestibular sense is crucial for a child's holistic development and wellbeing. It is important for babies and children to have a wide range of opportunities to stimulate and refine their vestibular sense, by experiencing movement such as rocking, spinning, twisting, turning, jumping, bouncing, wobbling, and moving at different speeds. Physically active play is the best way for babies and children to gain these experiences. We will discuss the relationship between play and children wellbeing and development in detail in chapter 5.

Proprioceptive sense

Proprioception is another lesser-known sense; it means 'the perception of oneself'. This sense is the awareness of where each part of our body is in space. For instance, when we walk through a doorway, our proprioceptive sense enables us to adjust our body position in relation to the door frame and navigate our body past someone coming in the opposite direction. This sense functions through tiny proprioceptors located in muscles, tensons and joints, which send signals to the nervous system which are integrated with information from other sensory systems, including the vestibular sense and vision (Tuthill and Azim, 2018).

Proprioception develops during early childhood, meaning that we quickly discover how much effort, or force to apply to complete a movement in everyday life. For example, as you pick up a cup of coffee, you know how tightly to grasp the cup, how heavy it is likely to be, how to move the cup to your mouth, and how much to tilt the cup in relation to the quantity of liquid it holds. When a child's proprioceptive sense is not well developed, they might appear clumsy or appear not to understand the idea of 'personal space'. However, for most children, it is a sense that develops with practice, so babies and young children need lots of opportunities to move in different environments, and to reach for and grasp objects. Making sure children have opportunities for pushing, pulling, lifting, digging and steering, for example, stimulates and develops this sense.

The signals the brain receives from these seven senses (and some other lesser-known senses) integrate to provide us with information about our surroundings and our bodies. It is through the senses that babies and young children learn about the world around them, come to recognise those who care for them, and build relationships with others. However, to really develop and sharpen these senses, babies and young children need lots and lots of opportunity to experience, explore and be active in different environments. The final section of this chapter looks at how knowledge of the body systems and senses can be used to enhance environments for babies' and young children's development and wellbeing.

TIME TO REFLECT

Before you go on to the next section, think about all the activities you do with children that help them develop an understanding of their senses. Do you focus more on some senses than others? Could you think about activities you could introduce to include those senses you have given less attention to?

The role of the environment

Sensory rich environments

One of the ways we can ensure that babies and young children have access to a wide range of sensory experiences is to reflect on the 'affordances', or opportunities in the environments they encounter.

The term 'affordance' was coined by American psychologist James J. Gibson (1977). Gibson was famous for his research on how children come to understand the world through their senses whilst they interact with the environment. The idea of 'affordance' helps us to consider how the environment can provide for, or indeed constrain, sensory development and holistic development in young children. Affordance theory illustrates how particular features of an object, or an environment can enable us to do something. Keenan and Evans (2009) have defined affordances as 'the properties of objects that offer the individual the potential to interact', and they describe how young children 'by moving about and exploring their environment, . . . come to understand which objects are best grasped, squeezed, tasted, or avoided' (p. 135). For example, a fallen tree trunk in the woods can be sat on, climbed on, balanced on, crawled on, stepped over (depending on its size), amongst other things – the tree trunk affords these actions which engaged children's senses of vision, hearing, touch, smell (and possibly taste), and their proprioceptive and vestibular senses. In essence, the tree trunk 'affords' these activities and the sensory experiences involved.

However, for the tree trunk to afford these actions, the child must firstly perceive the possibilities and secondly, must have the necessary skills to engage in the activity. Therefore, objects and environments have different affordances for different children. Whilst the tree trunk might afford climbing and balancing for an older, physically competent child, it affords exploration of texture for a 9-month-old (Little and Sweller, 2015).

However, Waters (2017) points out that action is not only afforded by the features of objects, but also by the rules and social norms of communities. For example, a playground slide affords being climbed up, but to avoid collisions with children sliding down, some nursery settings may prohibit children from climbing up the slide due to safety concerns.

Affordance theory is a useful tool for practitioner, or parents, to consider the environments they provide babies and young children, and the ways they allow these environments to be used, to reflect on the affordance for physical activity and sensory experiences.

TIME TO REFLECT

Think about an environment you know where young children engage in physical activity. Make a note of the affordances in that environment. How do the children engage with those affordances? Are there other ways that these affordances could be used? Could you support the children by introducing them to these ways?

The role of the adult

The role of the adult is a key factor which influences opportunities for young children to engage with the environment provided for developing these body systems and senses. This is particularly important if the environment is outdoors, as here adults can often become more passive in their role and see it as one of 'keeping an eye out'. Sometimes they may feel that just being outdoors is enough for the children in terms of their physical development. For example, in a study of two US settings, Dinkel et al. (2019) found that almost all the play (91%) was initiated by children with no adult input at all. Of course, it is important that children have opportunities to explore their environment independently but, given what we have learned about the body systems and senses so far, it is clear that the adult has an important role in ensuring that children's physical development is both supported and enhanced. Sometimes the adult not only forgets to do this, but they can actively prevent children engaging in ways that are beneficial for their physical development by discouraging interaction with certain affordances (Morrissey, Scott and Wishart, 2015) and by over-prioritising safety.

 # Observing

Before being able to effectively support and enhance children's learning in sensory rich environments, it is important that the adult can observe closely children's interactions with those environments. For example, if we think about outdoor interactions, Hall et al. (2014) highlight the importance of detailed and continual observation to understand what children do and how they behave so that 'a web of inter-related encounters' is supported. They also suggest that adults need to get on the same level as children to understand how they see the environment and interact with it, thereby encouraging an approach that is not just about observing the children but also observing the environment. It is also important to know what

Table 2.1 Observing children's physical activity

Do they engage...
in activities where their muscles have to work harder?
in activities where their heart rate increases?
in activities where they get out of breath?
in both large and small movements?
Are they gaining control over certain movements that they practise and refine?
Can they notice...
different smells in the environment?
different textures in the environment?
different sounds in the environment?
Do they...
notice if they are hot or cold?
move in response to music or rhythmic sounds?
point out small details in the environment?
crawl, walk, run, jump, climb, or skip freely?
have favourite tastes?
rock, spin, twist, turn, jump, bounce, wobble, move at different speeds, push, pull, lift, dig and steer?

to look for when observing children engaging in physical activity. In Table 2.1, we have listed some questions you could note responses to below as you consider physical activity, body systems and the role of the senses. Of course, you wouldn't be attempting to answer these in one short observation, but you could consider a child's activity over the space of a week for example. Their engagement with these actions will also depend on their age and development but it will give you a clear idea of what to look for, which in turn will give you ideas for activities you could introduce.

Supporting

Once you have observed the children, and have a good understanding of how they interact with the environment, you will want to consider your role and how you can best support them by:

i)   **providing** the most effective environment
ii) **modelling** actions and physical activity behaviours
iii) **consolidating** important physical skills.

Providing the most effective environment

Providing an effective environment is a key role of the adult; once you have been able to observe the children closely, as we have suggested above, you will be aware of their learning needs, where there are gaps in resources or opportunities, or where perhaps access to affordances is being restricted by over cautious adults. Macintyre (2012) reminds us of the importance of the first few years of a child's life. She cites Trevarthen (1977) who described how 'the young brain is thirsting for new information – we are powerless to control it' (p. 2). Macintyre goes on to recommend that 'practitioners [should] constantly strive to satisfy this urge by providing the best opportunities for learning' (p. 2). It is also a time when children are developing 'a sense of who they are and add to that their judgement of how able they are' (p.3). This is an important consideration – it is not just what children can do physically; it is what they think they can do. Does the environment you provide support them to answer internal questions such as:

Am I a physical person?
Am I good at moving my body?
Am I strong and competent?

Modelling

When you are happy with the environment you are providing for children to engage in physical development, then the next step is to consider your own behaviours within that environment. We talk about the idea of modelling to young children and this concept is just as pertinent when we are talking about physical activity. Modelling is when we don't give instructions to the children in terms of what they could do in an environment but rather we engage in behaviours that we would like them to copy. For example, I can model that it is best to stay inside when it is cold and wet, or I can model how to keep warm outside by running and jumping up and down. I could model how I interact with different affordances so that the children can choose to follow my lead.

Consolidating skills

Young children also need lots of opportunities to consolidate their rapidly developing physical skills, so they need to be able to return to the same activities again and again. They also need adults who can chunk learning into small steps if they notice a child is becoming frustrated with developing a certain skill. We often use the term 'scaffolding' to describe this kind of support and Fisher (2016, p. 14) reminds us of the importance of this concept and how 'the support of a skilled practitioner can be beneficial in helping the children to stay focused on an objective' and that 'scaffolding can . . . be highly appropriate when a practitioner is supporting a children to achieve their own outcomes in child-led situations'.

Enhancing

Children's ideas, imaginations and creativity can often astound us and when they are trusted to follow their own ideas and take the lead in their own learning, they show us how they understand their developmental needs and what they need to do to address them. This is as true of physical development as in all other areas of development. If you have observed the children closely, supported them in their learning and then returned to observation once more, you may realise that the effective environment you have provided is constraining them in some way, or at least not allowing the full possibilities of learning. Sometimes we just can't seem to keep up with the rapid nature of children's learning; this is why it is important to be continually appraising the environments we offer and to look for ways to enhance these. For example, Bjørgen (2016) found with 3–5-year-olds in Norway, that 'social possibilities and opportunities, human interactions, in the environment have the greatest influence on the duration and intensity of physically active play'. This suggests a need to consider how we can optimise those social possibilities if we want children to be as physically active as possible. If we think specifically about the outdoor environment, then there are certain features that can be included which will encourage greater physical activity. For example, Morrissey et al. (2015) demonstrated that 'the introduction of features such as edging, levels and inclines appeared to increase the level and variety of children's physical activity, and lead to greater utilization of the space' (p. 29). Ng et al. (2020), in the Australian context, discovered which environmental features might predict children's activity levels and these included grassy areas and the provision of balls.

It is clear from this section that what the adult does really matters. It matters that they **observe**, **support** and **enhance** continually, using each action to inform the other two.

TIME TO REFLECT

Think about how you support young children with their physical development; you may like to recall a recent occasion. What did you do? What did you provide? Observe? Model? Support? Enhance? As you note your response think about the areas of your practice you believe you need to develop.

CASE STUDY

In this case study Amy, a practitioner who works in an early years setting with young children aged 3–4 years, reflects on her practice, particularly in terms of what she has learnt about body systems, the senses and sensory rich environments. Read the case study and then consider how Amy's reflection may link to your own experiences of practice.

Amy decides that she tends to focus on observation and support and even then, she is more inclined to use observations to inform children's records rather than really engaging with a child on a deeper level through observation to see 'what they do' (Hall et al., 2014) and how they behave. She also wonders if she sometimes focuses on the kind of support that may constrain effective physical development; for example, she thinks about times that she uses 'hand holding' instead of supporting the child to find strategies to develop their confidence when they were climbing or playing at height. Amy decides to raise these points for discussion at a team meeting; the team discusses ways they could both develop the way they observe and support but also how they could use this knowledge to further model, as appropriate, and further enhance the physical environment for children in order to impact more effectively on their physical development.

Concluding thoughts

In this chapter, we have considered the importance of the body's systems and senses. We have also seen how important the environment is when we are thinking about young children's physical activity. It is the adult who provides this environment, but we have also asked you to consider other behaviours and practices that the adult should adopt. You have had lots of opportunity in this chapter to consider how you can apply this important subject knowledge to your practice. As you move forward with your practice, there are some top tips below to keep in mind.

Top tips

* **The unique child:** Individual children respond to sensory stimuli differently. We need to be sensitive to each child's reaction.
* **Role modelling:** Be a sensory role model! Comment on how things taste, what you can hear and how things feel.
* **Be curious:** Be alert to new and interesting sensory experiences.
* **Physical activity at the top of the agenda:** Remember that physical experience is important and necessary to support body systems.
* **A 'can-do' attitude**: Be positive and enjoy being active with children.

Key terms

Affordance	Explains how features of an environment can enable us to do something.
Circulatory system	The system responsible for moving blood throughout the body
Respiratory system	The system responsible for bringing oxygen into the body and expelling carbon dioxide.
Muscular-skeletal system	A complex network of bones, joints, muscles, ligaments, and tendons, that work together to provide support and enable the body to move.
Nervous system	A complex network of cells that transmit signals between different parts of the body.
Vestibular sense	Sense of balance
Proprioceptive sense	Sense of space
Sensory integration	How the brain integrates and organises the information produced by the senses.
Auditory system	The system that enables us to hear.
Retina	The curved part of the eye which sends messages to the brain.

In the next chapter you will be introduced to further ideas about how to develop and support young children's movement skills. The focus will be on both fine and gross motor skills; we will look at how they are defined and explain why they are important, outlining how these skills can be supported in early childhood settings. We will think about how these skills link to learning and holistic development and explore some of the barriers that can compromise their acquisition, rehearsal and refinement. We will also continue to consider the importance of the environment, making links with your learning from this chapter.

 ## Further reading

Gascoyne, S. (2013) *Sensory Play: Play in the EYFS* 2nd Edition, Practical Pre-School Books.

Louis, S. (2022) *Observing Young Children: A Froebelian Approach.* London: The Froebel Trust.

The School Run – Learning about the Human Body. Available at: https://www.theschoolrun.com/learning-about-body-primary-school

References

Bjørgen, K. (2016) 'Physical activity in light of affordances in outdoor environments: qualitative observation studies of 3–5 years olds in kindergarten', *SpringerPlus*, 5(1), p. 950. doi:10.1186/s40064-016-2565-y

Cournoyer, M., Gauthier, A.C., Maldera, A., Maso, F.D. and Mathieu, M.E. (2022) 'Effect of physical activity on olfactory acuity: A systematic review', *medRxiv*, pp. 2022–2009.

Day, B.L. and Fitzpatrick, R.C. (2005) 'The vestibular system', *Current Biology*, 15(15), pp. 583–586.

Dinkel, D., Snyder, K., Patterson, T., Warehime, S., Kuhn, M. and Wisneski, D. (2019) 'An exploration of infant and toddler unstructured outdoor play', *European Early Childhood Education Research Journal* 27 (2), pp. 257–271.

Field, T. (2010) 'Touch for socioemotional and physical well-being: A review', *Developmental Review*, 30(4), pp. 367–383.

Fisher, J. (2016) *Interacting or Interfering? Improving Interactions in the Early Years.* Maidenhead: OUP.

Gibson, J. (1977) 'The theory of affordances', in R. Shaw and J. Bransford (eds), *Perceiving, Acting, and Knowing: Toward an Ecological Psychology*, pp. 67–82. Hillsdale, NJ: Erlbaum.

Hall, E., Linnea Howe, S., Roberts, S., Foster Shaffer, L. and Williams, E. 2014. 'What can we learn through careful observation of infants and toddlers in nature?', *Children, Youth & Environments* 24 (2), pp. 192–214.

Keenan, T. and Evans, S. (2009) *An Introduction to Child Development*. London: Sage.

Little, H. and Sweller, N. (2015) 'Affordances for risk-taking and physical activity in Australian early childhood education settings', *Early Childhood Education Journal*, 43(4), pp. 337–345. doi:10.1007/s10643-014-0667-0.

Macintyre, C. (2012) *Understanding Babies and Young Children from Conception to Three*. Abingdon: Routledge.

Morrissey, A., Scott, C. and Wishart, L. (2015) 'Infant and toddler responses to a redesign of their childcare outdoor play space', *Children, Youth & Environments*, 25(1), pp. 29–56.

Ng. M., Rosenberg, M., Thornton, A., Lester, L., Trost, S.G., Bai, P., Christian, H. (2020) 'The Effect of Upgrades to Childcare Outdoor Spaces on Preschoolers' Physical Activity: Findings from a Natural Experiment', *Int J Environ Res Public Health*. Jan 10;17(2):468. doi: 10.3390/ijerph17020468. PMID: 31936783; PMCID: PMC7014450.

Pocock, G., Richards, C.D. and Richards, D.A. (2013) *Human Physiology*. Oxford: Oxford University Press.

Sherwood, L. (2015) *Human Physiology: From Cells to Systems*. Cengage Learning.

Tuthill, J.C. and Azim, E. (2018). 'Proprioception', *Current Biology*. 28 (5): 194–203. doi:10.1016/j.cub.2018.01.064

Waters, J. (2017), 'Affordance theory in outdoor play', in Waller, T., Ärlemalm-Hagsér, E., Sandseter, E. B., Lee-Hammond, L., Lekies, K. and Wyver, S. (eds), *The SAGE handbook of Outdoor Play and Learning*, pp. 40–54.

Winberg, J. and Porter, R.H. (1998) 'Olfaction and human neonatal behaviour: Clinical implications', *Acta Paediatrica*, 87(1), pp. 6–10.

Supporting physical development in children

The current state of babies' and children's physical development and activity

Ben Langdown

Introduction

A core role of practitioners in early childhood education and care settings is to effectively support children in the development of movement skills. This is not confined to the early childhood practitioner and indeed, parents and others living or working with children have the perfect opportunity to support this development too. Within these roles, goals are often set to develop physical competence in many of the basic movements required in early childhood. Achieving these will support the child's next stage of development. Indeed, simply knowing how much physical activity is recommended for children, and how to facilitate this, can promote effective support and movement development.

Not only does physical activity link to movement competency, but also to children's learning and holistic development. By defining motor skills and highlighting the role movement can play in supporting an overall smooth development of health, wellbeing, and learning, you can reflect on how

DOI: 10.4324/9781003386728-3

physical literacy can be fostered in early childhood settings. Barriers can, and do, exist that may compromise motor skill acquisition, rehearsal, and refinement. Promoting creativity, focusing on the individual's needs, and establishing a movement culture within the environment may allow these barriers to be overcome. This chapter has a particular emphasis on defining movement skills, observing them and identifying how best to support and foster an environment in which physical development can thrive.

How much physical activity do young children need?

The World Health Organization (WHO) (2019) state that replacing time children spend in restrained positions (for example, bouncers/walkers) or engaged in sedentary screen time with moderate- to vigorous-intensity physical activity can provide health benefits, especially where sleep quality and quantity are preserved. Highlighting the benefits of physical activity allows justification of why it is vital to support physical development from birth. In the UK, we can draw on the Chief Medical Officers' (CMO) Physical Activity Guidelines (2019) to inform us of the current activity guidelines.

Some highlights from CMO (UK) Physical Activity Guidelines (UK Chief Medical Officers, 2019) include:

Children aged 1 to 5 years: aim for at least 180 minutes per day; activities could include: playground, jumping, climbing, messy play, throwing and catching, skipping, object play, dancing, games, playing, swimming, walking, using a scooter, riding a bike, etc.

Under 1s should have at least 30 minutes activity across the day (for example, tummy time).

Disabled children should start integrating daily physical activity slowly. Where possible, the CMO recommend building up from bite-size chunks of physical activity to 20 mins per day to achieve good health benefits. Children should also attempt challenging, but manageable strength and balancing activities three times per week (UK Chief Medical Officer, 2022).

You should note that, in contrast to the World Health Organisation's (WHO) (2019) recommendations, the UK CMO do not currently provide recommendations for sedentary time or sleep.

This information was correct at time of publication; however, new guidelines can be searched for using 'CMO physical activity guidelines' as the search term.

Figure 3.1 WHO Physical Activity Guidelines
Reproduced with the permission of the World Health Organization,
https://www.who.int/health-topics/physical-activity
World Health Organization (2019) *Guidelines on Physical Activity, Sedentary Behaviour and Sleep for Children under 5 Years of Age*. World Health Organization.
https://apps.who.int/iris/handle/10665/311664 License: CC BY-NC-SA 3.0 IGO

TIME TO REFLECT

How much time did you spend playing outside as a child? Do you remember what activities you took part in?

CASE STUDY

COVID-19

Events from recent years (during COVID-19 pandemic restrictions) caused a shift in the amount of physical activity some children have been exposed to. Research found that even a year on from the last lockdown (January–March 2021) only small increases in the amount of children achieving the 60 minutes of moderate to vigorous physical activity were seen (37% up to 41% in 2022) (Jago et al., 2023). However, the environment and participation history of the family / child can also impact upon levels of physical activity (Yomoda and Kurita, 2021). Families with more space at home, or with a history of increased physical activity were more likely to experience less decreases during COVID-19 restrictions. Furthermore, older children were more likely to see reductions in physical activity vs younger children. Boys were more likely to remain active, but if they did cut back, then they saw larger reductions compared to girls (Yomoda and Kurita, 2021). Online content viewing increased in many countries during COVID-19 restrictions, but increases are also seen during school holidays (Lozano-Blasco et al., 2021). It is therefore important to offer families other options beyond the screen to support physical development and exploration of movement in varying environments, especially as parents' support and encouragement are often positively associated with increased physical activity in young children (Yomoda and Kurita, 2021).

The benefits of physical activity

There has never been a more pressing time to support the development of young children's movement with the aim of them engaging in physical activity for life. You only have to look at the latest National Child Measurement Programme (NHS, 2022) to see the importance of this. The 2021/22 report highlights that 22.2% of children in Reception (aged 4–5 years), and 37.7% of children in Year 6 (aged 10–11 years) are classed as either overweight or obese. Rising obesity levels, coupled with ever-younger children favouring technology use over outdoor play, is contributing to these current statistics, and these are predicted to rise to 66% of all 2–15-year-olds in the UK by 2050 (Government Office for Science, 2007). The decline of outdoor play during childhood can be associated with reduced physical activity (Slutsky and DeShetler, 2017) and competence when it comes to fundamental movement skills (FMS) (that is, the ability to complete foundation/basic learnt movement patterns that do not occur naturally and are suggested to be the building blocks for more complex activities. Fundamental movement skills can be categorised into locomotion, manipulation and stabilisation skills that are used in play and everyday life) (Barnett et al., 2016).

Examples

Locomotion skills: Running, skipping, hopping, rolling, etc.
Manipulation (object control) skills: Catching, throwing, kicking, striking, etc.
Stabilisation skills: Balancing, landing, turning, bracing, etc.

An Active Lives Survey (Sport England, 2018) highlighted that schools are not providing adequate opportunities to achieve the UK CMO (2019) and WHO (2019) recommended 60 minutes of moderate to vigorous physical activity each day, with only 19.6% of ~1.39 million children achieving this target. The Gateshead Millennium Study (Farooq et al., 2018) also found that there was a drop in physical activity levels at 7 years of age, which is concerning for both physical and mental health, children's learning, socialisation and motivation to partake in physical activity across the life span.

However, as Agans et al. (2013) suggest, we should not just be concerned with 'Is there physical activity?', 'how much?', and 'over what period?'. Instead, fostering a culture within early years settings where children are encouraged to be active and be subject to positive movement experiences throughout the day, could lead to a movement culture that both achieves these targets and recognises the child's lived experiences within the movement context (Agans et al., 2013; Langdown, 2021).

Physical literacy

As young children progress towards school age, much emphasis is placed upon the 'core' subjects of phonics, reading, writing, and mathematics. Whilst becoming literate in these areas is undoubtedly important from a quality-of-life perspective, being physically active and developing 'physical literacy' is arguably the only literacy that can have a *direct* impact on health and life expectancy. Physical literacy is an important concept that has attracted a lot of research and attention in recent years. As Bailey (2021) states, there are many definitions of physical literacy, and some focus purely on the development of movement skills, whereas others take a more holistic approach with a focus on motivation to maintain a lifelong goal of physical activity. Being physically literate allows children to take part in sport or physical activity with a degree of competence when they are older, hopefully leading to confidence, motivation and a desire to continue participating in physical activity, sport or fitness pursuits throughout their life. Although research tells us that movement skills are an important part of physical literacy, being able to interpret and interact with the physical environment, develop social interactions and develop underpinning knowledge of the values of physical activity for health and wellbeing are also important components. One such definition, that posits physical literacy as a combination of movement competency elements and the psychosocial and cognitive elements, is:

> As appropriate to each individual, physical literacy can be described as the motivation, confidence, physical competence, knowledge and understanding to value and take responsibility for engaging in physical activity for life.
>
> (Whitehead, 2019, p. 8)

While physical literacy may not be achieved in the first five years, this specific definition does stress the important role early years practitioners and parents have in supporting the development of movement opportunities and fostering the confidence and motivation to engage across the lifespan. This can ultimately lead to competence in physical skills as well as the confidence and motivation to manage the school day, and independently achieve physical tasks.

TIME TO REFLECT

Can you recall who provided support and facilitated your motivation to engage in physical activity?

How did they go about this and are you still engaged in physical activity now?

What can you learn from this to support children towards physical literacy in your current setting?

Why physical activity is important for young children

We know that now is an important time to foster a movement culture into the lives of children through the environments in which they engage. Physical activity is as important for a baby as it is for toddlers, children, adolescents and into adulthood. Young children love to be as active as possible, moving around freely. For babies, the benefits come from unrestricted floor-based activity, helping them to develop the physical strength necessary for lifting their heads, rolling, and into crawling. This leads to good posture, stability, spatial awareness and the development of movement patterns. Alongside this, floor-based movement helps them to maintain a healthy weight and to develop their senses and early language and communication through social interactions with parents, carers, siblings, etc.

For toddlers and pre-school children, it's important to continue fostering their love of physical activity because the benefits here can be seen through the development of fundamental movement skills, the building blocks for movement, which are transferable to other physical activity, sport and fitness pursuits throughout life. In response to physical activity, a child's bones and muscles will get stronger, their heart and lungs will adapt, increasing fitness levels and maintaining healthy weight (Pate et al., 2019), plus they will also develop socially and emotionally through interaction with others and their environment (Borland et al., 2022). In fact, there is research showing that physical activity can support the development of brain structures (Ortega et al., 2019), social interaction and communication skills (Zhao and Chen, 2018) and an increase in self-confidence, motivation and retention of information.

Autism and attention deficit hyperactivity disorder (ADHD)

Regular, structured exercise sessions targeting social interaction and communication were undertaken by a group of 5–8-year-old children diagnosed as autistic. Following the sessions the children showed significantly increased communication, cooperation, social interaction, and self-control (Zhao and Chen, 2018).

A study by Chan et al. (2022) examined the research around physical activity for children with Attention Deficit Hyperactivity Disorder (ADHD). The review concluded that employing exercise programmes for children with ADHD that include moderate-high intensity physical activity and cognitive tasks (for example, using movement planning skills) is suitable to facilitate increased self-confidence and improve communication and social interaction skills.

Both single-bout and long-term exercises can improve the blood flow to the brain, enhance information processing capacity and attention, decrease impulsiveness, and increase inhibitory control, thereby improving interpersonal relationships.

(Chan et al., 2022)

Above all, fostering an environment in which physical activity is encouraged and a core, valued aspect of the day-to-day structure, will help children form positive associations with physical activity (Agans et al., 2013), hopefully leading to immediate and long-term health benefits and physically active lives.

How can you support physical development?

Physical skills play a critical role in supporting the overall development of children from a health and wellbeing perspective through to their learning and academic achievements. Indeed, the British Heart Foundation (2019) state that we learn more physical skills during the first five years of our lives than at any other time. It is therefore vital that time and opportunities to practice and develop are provided to support these physical skills. The acquisition, rehearsing and refinement of movement skills should be an organic element of every child's day, whether at home, nursery or at school. You will consider these environments further in Chapter 4.

In order to support a child's development towards physical literacy it is important that you are aware of the phases that children will move through. It is argued, that being physically literate involves more than just being able to move effectively. In practice, it is also about children being provided with the opportunities to overcome movement challenges (Pot et al., 2017).

 TIME TO REFLECT

What movement opportunities do you provide to children in your setting? How do you ensure there are new learning opportunities through their movement?

The ABCs of movement

As babies develop into toddlers and on into young children, they build upon their existing acquisition of movements. Gross movements (or 'motor skills') are developed first, which then allows the smaller more refined movements (called 'fine motor skills') to be learnt and put into action.

Gross motor skills definition

Skills performed using large parts of the body (or even the whole body) and requiring less precision are classified as gross motor skills, for example, crawling or running safely.

Fine motor skills definition

Skills that require greater precision in the control of small muscles are classified as fine motor skills, for example, grasping an object.

Put simply, gross motor skills are the big body movements that most children, regardless of gender, ethnicity, culture, or environment, will develop in roughly the same order over a similar period of time. The development of these FMS provides increased strength, agility, balance, and coordination to learn more complex movement skills as children grow and develop. Competent execution of FMS ensure children are able to play and move safely and securely in all environments when being physically active.

Being confident and competent movers has a positive effect on the development of their communication and language through play. The forming of long-term friendships is helped by being able to join in, keep up, and contribute ideas. And their physical health, wellbeing and development is properly supported through daily experience of a range of movement opportunities.

(Manners, 2023)

It is important to note that FMS usually emerge in a specific order, but that the rate of development, the confidence and movement competence depends on the learning environment, the opportunities children are provided with and the motivation they have to learn. Children often skip movement 'milestones' and catch up later through spikey or uneven (known as asynchronous) development. This is usually of little concern and as such the organic process of acquiring movement skills should be supported through the infusion of the movement culture discussed later in this chapter and previously presented (Langdown, 2021). It is worth noting that children with Down syndrome often experience delays in motor milestones (Haywood and Getchell, 2021).

Which movements, when?

Without strong roots, beautiful plants may not flourish and grow.
(Manners, 2023)

When babies are born, they are able to do a few things: breathe, cry, suck and move their legs in alternating patterns (Haywood and Getchell, 2021). As we are aware, this does not mean that they are able to walk straight away! With time they acquire and refine FMS, strength and stability. These skills are vital to their development towards overall locomotion, object control and stabilisation.

Expert opinion:

Even babies in the womb are continually practising their movement skills. All the vigorous kicks and pummels, squirming, and wiggling are really important as they explore their watery environment, communicate likes and dislikes, and get themselves in the right position to be born, often a massive physical effort for both mother and baby. The first year of a child's life is all about laying down firm physical foundations so that, at every developmental stage, a new skill can be seamlessly added to those already evident. So practising rolling over front to back, back to front, gives babies the strength needed to lie on their tummies and push up on their hands. At some point, they will get onto their hands and knees and start to crawl. This is the most brilliant whole-body workout. They have to be balanced, coordinated, agile, and strong to move in different directions around obstacles and at different speeds. All the strength, balance, and coordination gained at this point goes towards being able to sit independently, then stand, then start to walk.

What we need to remember is that all movement experience is of enormous value, and that standing or sitting still is one of the most physically challenging things for children to do. Practising the big-body gross motor skills, like rolling, crawling, climbing, walking, running, and jumping, must not be forgotten just because they've moved on to other activities that are more complex and demanding.

By ensuring the pelvic and shoulder girdles are stable, more complex, manipulative, or fine motor skills may be learned. Pelvic stability means children's core strength is well enough developed to ensure they can sit still on a chair for a few minutes at a time to listen and concentrate. Likewise, shoulder stability affects the stability at the elbow and wrist joints that, in turn, will determine how easily and fluently they engage with writing and drawing materials. It is really important to remember that all the fine motor or manipulative skills, like cutting, threading, modelling, writing, painting, and drawing, are completely dependent on reliable gross motor skills.

(Manners, 2023)

Being able to identify what FMS individual babies, toddlers and young children should be acquiring through rehearsal and refinement at specific ages is useful to all those supporting physical development.

Remember that these are a rough guide to gross motor development and that each individual child may vary from this order – especially when considering children with special educational needs and disabilities (SEND). When babies and young children are learning the gross FMS, it is important to note that they do not need to be forced into actions, for example, sitting up, crawling, or walking. Supporting walking and jumping through the use of baby walkers or jumpers for example is not required for them to learn these FMS and can in fact compromise their smooth emergence/acquisition.

Table 3.1 Example of gross and fine motor skill development timeline

Gross Motor Skills	Fine Motor Skills
0–6 months	**3–6 months**
Lifting head	Uses both hands to reach for and grasp objects. Will occasionally use one hand
Rolling	**6–12 months**
Sitting (with support)	Uses pincer grasp with thumb and index finger
6–12 months	Transfers objects from one hand to the other
Crawling on stomach	**1–2 years**
Sitting (without support)	Picks up small objects quickly using fine pincer grasp
Stands with support and walks holding on	Turns two or three pages of a book at a time
Rolls a ball	Holds pencil at middle or top with whole hand or attempt at thumb and fingers grip
12–18 months	Scribbles
Crawling	Beginning to show favoured hand
Walks alone	**2–3 years**
18 months–2 years	Starts to hold pencil near point and uses thumb and fingers grip
Walks smoothly and turns corners	Can turn single pages in a book
Walks upstairs with support	Can snip with toy scissors
Begins running	Eats without assistance
2–3 years	**3–4 years**
Walks upstairs without support	Manipulates clay material (rolls a ball, makes snakes, pancakes)
Runs safely	Can build a tower of up to ten blocks using both hands cooperatively
Catches using body and arms	Can use pencil with proper grip and control, like an adult and can copy circles
3–4 years	**4–5 years**
Kicks a ball forwards	Can draw squares, write the numbers 1–5 and copy letters
Can hop on one foot	Dresses and undresses independently

Gross Motor Skills	Fine Motor Skills
4–5 years	
Catches using only their hands	
Can skip following a demonstration	

Note: Remember that these are a rough guide to gross and fine motor development and that each individual child may vary from this order – especially when considering children with special educational needs and disabilities (SEND).

Supporting the development of movement

When supporting the development of FMS, it is not necessary to teach skills in isolation. In fact, FMS can and should be acquired organically through play, experimenting in different environments, contexts and under various task constraints or guided play activities.

> Get Strong. Move More. Break up inactivity.
>
> (UK Chief Medical Officers, 2019)

By breaking up inactivity you will help to ensure that you are supporting physical development and allowing children to reach the target of 180 minutes of physical activity per day. Periods of physical activity provide many valuable opportunities for you to observe and effectively gather information about an individual child's movement development needs.

Movements will be learnt best through the creation of a culture where movement is infused into the early years setting, celebrated and often presenting positive challenges to the children. Through such movement cultures, you should aim to establish a child's level of physical development as early as possible and monitor over the course of time that is spent supporting that individual child (that is weeks, months, years). It is only through time that disciplined and systematically focused observations of the critical features of each FMS can take place. The observer must themselves learn the skill of observation and analysis to become effective at identifying the development needs of each child more efficiently (Hayward and Getchell, 2014).

To apply appropriate support/interventions, practitioners, parents and others need to know what they are observing when attempting to assess the level of development already achieved by individual babies/children. As highlighted, it is useful therefore, to be able to identify the critical features of FMS before trying to observe and assess the stage of development a child is at. It is worth noting that the development of a movement is not a linear process; it can be spikey and can involve setbacks and periods where little improvement is seen, especially during phases of rapid growth. Progress can often emerge in another developmental domain, for example, new friendships/use of language/practising the sequencing of skills through play, etc.

CASE STUDY

FMS: throwing

Below are some of the critical movement features of a developed throwing action:

- A long contralateral step – i.e. stepping forwards with the opposite foot to the throwing arm over a distance of more than half the child's standing height.
- The throwing arm rotates backwards as the step is taken.
- The trunk rotates forward to add force to the throw.
- The throwing arm comes forward as, or just after the trunk rotates to a front-facing position. This creates lag in the arm to create more force in the throw.

 TIME TO REFLECT

Now consider the movements involved in a well-developed crawling action and a well-developed jumping action. Can you identify what you would see as the top 3 or 4 critical movement features in each of these FMS?

Fostering and stifling creativity

How often have you observed a child tripping over, falling off their bike, not quite landing a jump, running into another child or object? Without mistakes children would not learn; without appropriate celebration of those mistakes they would be reluctant to try again.

TIME TO REFLECT

Consider a child climbing onto and along a small wall. What would you say to them? Would you tell them to 'be careful'? Would you encourage their exploration and risk taking while ensuring their safety? Or would you say nothing and lift them off the wall?

It is useful to reflect on the feedback you provide children within any setting and how that feedback or 'off the cuff comment' could impact upon their motivation, confidence, risk taking and ultimately FMS competence. Here are some top tips for using effective feedback and dialogue with children to develop movement creativity:

- Celebrate mistakes, encourage them to try again, find another way, ask a friend to demonstrate/support.
- Encourage free play for creative exploration of movement to emerge.
- Develop varying constraints on tasks and play based scenarios to guide specific movement development. For example, setting an obstacle course on play equipment where they will have to use crawling actions, climbing and balance skills, and be tasked with hopping across a certain area. Where children are struggling, make the task (in this case, the obstacle course) easier, and where children are competent, increase the level of challenge – this helps to maintain motivation, engagement with the tasks and confidence.
- Consider adult attitudes/feedback towards movement and the use of 'off the cuff comments' that limit risk taking and stifle creativity in movement (for example, 'be careful', 'don't run' and 'you might fall' – but they *might* not and these words have then stopped risk taking and stifled a positive movement development opportunity!).

- Engage your child(ren) in movement in all appropriate environments. It doesn't have to be anything complicated or expensive, just involve fun and movement!
- Ensure that movement is at the heart of the majority of activities (remember: break up inactivity) and that everyone in the setting buys into this to foster a movement culture and many positive movement experiences for babies and children of all ages.

Supporting the individual child

Earlier in this chapter, we saw how FMS can be observed and used as feedback to provide support for movement development. However, it may not always be appropriate to provide an intervention at that specific time for that individual child. The child may have their own views on what they'd like to play, achieve, or indeed what they consider they struggle with (for example, ball skills, swinging across the monkey-bars, climbing). Furthermore, you may see that there is a need to develop their movement for specific reasons in their setting (for example, safety/socialisation/to aid language development, etc.). By infusing movement into the culture of any early years setting you are in, it is possible for positive movement experiences, alongside listening to the child voice, to organically highlight the areas children want and need support with. Forcing movement may lead to specific foci being targeted for development, which contradicts the notion of meeting the individual's holistic needs.

 TIME TO REFLECT

In the final reflections of this chapter, consider the two points below:

Reflection 1: Can you describe three ways in which your environment supports physical development and describe three things you would like to do differently/change having read this chapter?

Reflection 2: Choose a movement skill from each age group you care for and describe how you could support/enhance the development of this over time, in your setting.

Concluding thoughts

Children will all grow and develop at different rates. Some may skip some stages of motor skill development; others may progress and regress at different points or show development in other areas (for example, emotional and social development). One thing is for sure, supporting them with opportunities to explore, take measured risks, and helping them to learn new skills will provide them with many physical and mental benefits for their childhood and beyond into adulthood. As a practitioner, parent or carer of children, it's important to understand how gross and fine motor skills are related, how they can be developed and how observing movement can allow you to support each individual child's needs. Fostering an environment in which children can thrive and benefit from positive movement experiences will ensure you are able to support their development effectively towards the goal of physical literacy.

Top tips

- Be aware that all children develop at different rates – age is the least useful indicator when considering physical skills.
- Physical skills do not need to be forced in any way – remember that constraint-based supports may in fact compromise their development, for example, baby-walkers.
- You don't need specialist equipment to encourage children to move – just a clean floor when babies and then space outside when older.
- Acknowledge the benefits of how early positive movement experiences can impact on later successful engagement with physical activity.
- Remember that while FMS are the cornerstones to becoming physically literate, progression does not occur in a linear fashion and that progress may come in the form of other domains.
- Bear in mind the UK Chief Medical Officers' guidelines with the goal of supporting children to achieve 180 minutes of physical activity per day – 'Get Strong. Move More. Break up inactivity.'

Reading for children

Andreade, G. (2014) *Giraffes Can't Dance*. Orchard Books. A book aimed at encouraging a playful approach to movement for very young children.
John, J. and Oswald, P. (2021) *The Couch Potato*. HarperCollins. Part of a series of books aimed at 4- to 8-year-olds.

References

Agans, J.P., Säfvenbom, R., Davis, J.L., Bowers, E.P. and Lerner, R.M. (2013) 'Positive movement experiences: Approaching the study of athletic participation, exercise, and leisure activity through relational developmental systems theory and the concept of embodiment', *Advances in Child Development and Behavior*, 45, pp. 261–286. doi:10.1016/B978-0-12-397946-9.00010-5

Bailey, R. (2021) 'Defining physical literacy: Making sense of a promiscuous concept, *Sport in Society*, 25(1), pp. 163–180. doi:10.1 080/17430437.2020.1777104

Barnett, L.M., Stodden, D., Cohen, K.E., Smith, J.J., Lubans, D.R., Lenoir, M., Livonen, S., Miller, A.D., Laukkanen, A., Dudley, D., Lander, N.J., Brown, H. and Morgan, P.J. (2016) 'Fundamental movement skills: An important focus', *Journal of Teaching in Physical Education*, 35(3), pp. 219–225. doi:10.1123/jtpe.2014-0209

Borland, R.L., Cameron, L. A., Tonge, B. J. and Gray, K. M. (2022). 'Effects of physical activity on behaviour and emotional problems, mental health and psychosocial well-being in children and adolescents with intellectual disability: A systematic review', *Journal of Applied Research in Intellectual Disabilities*, 35(2), 399–420. doi:10.1111/jar.12961

British Heart Foundation (2019) *Booklet 2: Early Movers – Helping Under-5s Live Active & Healthy Lives: Introduction to Physical Activity in the Early Years.* Available at: https://soscn.org/downloads /resources/early_movers/Booklet_2_Introduction_to_physical_ activity_in_the_early_years.pdf (Accessed 24 August 2023.)

Chan, Y.S., Jang, J.T. and Ho, C.S. (2022) 'Effects of physical exercise on children with attention deficit hyperactivity disorder', *Biomedical Journal*, 45(2), 265–270. doi:10.1016/j.bj.2021.11.011

Farooq, M.A., Parkinson, K.N., Adamson, A.J., Pearce, M.S., Reilly, J.K., Hughes, A.R., Janssen, X., Basterfield, L. and Reilly, J.J. (2018) 'Timing of the decline in physical activity in childhood and adolescence: Gateshead Millennium Cohort Study', *British Journal of Sports Medicine*, 52(15), 1002–1006. doi:10.1136/bjsports-2016-096933

Government Office for Science (2007) *Tackling Obesities: Future Choices – Project Report* (2nd edn). Foresight. Available at: https://assets.publishing.service.gov.uk/media/5a759da7e5274a4 368298a4f/07-1184x-tackling-obesities-future-choices-report.pdf (Accessed 24 August 2023.)

Haywood, K.M. and Getchell, N. (2021) *Life Span Motor Development* (7th edn). Harrogate, UK: Human Kinetics.

Jago, R., Salway, R., House, D., Walker, R., Emm-Collison, L., Sansum, K., Breheny, K., Reid, T., Churchward, S., Williams, J. G., Foster, C., Hollingworth, W. and de Vocht, F. (2023) 'Short and medium-term effects of the COVID-19 lockdowns on child and parent accelerometer-measured physical activity and sedentary time: a natural experiment', *The International Journal of Behavioral Nutrition and Physical Activity*, 20(1), 42. doi:10.1186/s12966-023-01441-1

Langdown, B. (2021) Developing a movement culture in the first ten years, in Bailey, R., Agans, J.P., Côté, J., Daly-Smith, A. and Tomporowski, P. (eds) *Physical Activity and Sport During the First Ten Years of Life: Multidisciplinary Perspectives* (pp. 188–203). doi:10.4324/9780429352645-20

Lozano-Blasco, R., Quilez-Robres, A., Delgado-Bujedo, D. and Latorre-Martínez, M.P. (2021). 'YouTube's growth in use among children

0–5 during COVID19: The Occidental European case', *Technology in Society*, 66, 101648. doi:10.1016/j.techsoc.2021.101648

Manners, L. (2023) Audio recording in Week 3, Supporting the development of children's movement skills, in Supporting physical Development in Early Childhood. Available at https://www.open.edu/openlearn/health-sports-psychology/supporting-physical-development-early-childhood?active-tab=description-tab (Accessed 15 January 2024).

NHS (2022) National Child Measurement Programme, England, *2021/2 School Year*. Available at: https://digital.nhs.uk/data-and-information/publications/statistical/national-child-measurement-programme/2021-22-school-year (Accessed 24 August 2023.)

Ortega, F.B., Campos, D., Cadenas-Sanchez, C., Altmäe, S., Martínez-Zaldívar, C., Martín-Matillas, M., Catena, A. and Campoy, C. (2019) 'Physical fitness and shapes of subcortical brain structures in children', *British Journal of Nutrition*, 122(s1), S49–S58. doi:10.1017/S0007114516001239

Pate, R.R., Hillman, C.H., Janz, K.F., Katzmarzyk, P.T., Powell, K.E., Torres, A. and Whitt-Glover, M.C. (2019) 'Physical activity and health in children younger than 6 years: A systematic review', *Medicine and Science in Sports and Exercise*, 51(6), 1282–1291. doi:10.1249/MSS.0000000000001940

Pot, N., van Hilvoorde, I., Afonso, J., Koekoek, J. and Almond, L. (2017) 'Meaningful movement behaviour involves more than the learning of fundamental movement skills', *International Sports Studies*, 39(2), 5–20. doi:10.30819/iss.39-2.02

Slutsky, R. and DeShetler, L.M. (2017) 'How technology is transforming the ways in which children play', *Early Child Development and Care*, 187(7), 1138–1146. doi:10.1080/03004430.2016.1157790

Sport England (2018) *Active Lives – Children and Young People Survey*. December, 1–34. Available at: https://www.sportengland.org/media/13698/active-lives-children-survey-academic-year-17-18.pdf (Accessed 24 August 2023.)

UK Chief Medical Officer (2022) *Physical Activity for Disabled Children and Disabled Young People.* Available at: https://www.gov.uk/government/publications/physical-activity-in-disabled-children-and-disabled-young-people-evidence-review (Accessed 24 August 2023.)

UK Chief Medical Officers (CMO) (2019) *UK Chief Medical Officers ' Physical Activity Guidelines.* September, 1–65. Available at: https://www.gov.uk/government/publications/physical-activity-guidelines-uk-chief-medical-officers-report (Accessed 24 August 2023.)

World Health Organization (WHO) (2019) *WHO Guidelines: Physical Activity, Sedentary Behavior and Sleep for Children under 5 Years of Age.* doi:10.1055/a-1489-8049 (Accessed 24 August 2023.)

Yomoda, K. and Kurita, S. (2021) 'Influence of social distancing during the COVID-19 pandemic on physical activity in children: A scoping review of the literature', *Journal of Exercise Science and Fitness,* 19(3), 195–203. doi:10.1016/j.jesf.2021.04.002

Zhao, M. andChen, S. (2018) 'The effects of structured physical activity program on social interaction and communication for children with autism', *BioMed Research International,* 2018. doi:10.1155/2018/1825046

Movement and learning

Joanne Josephidou

Introduction

We have seen so far how important physical activity is for young children's health, physical development and wellbeing. Yet this is only half the story; there are also important links to be made between young children's learning and their opportunities to move. When we consider the best pedagogies for the early years, we must remember that movement is vital for children; it is 'central to young children's learning' (Bilton, 2004, p. 92). As we discovered in the previous chapter, children need the right environment and supportive adults to help them develop both gross and fine motor skills as they grow and learn. In this chapter, we explore in more detail the links between children moving and children learning. We have already highlighted the typical sequence of movements for children from birth to 5 years old and that there are key milestones we can look out for; in this chapter we build on this knowledge.

At the same time as acknowledging these milestones, we recognise the importance of considering each child as unique and we want to promote the understanding that they will develop in their own way and their own time. We continue to stress in this chapter that it is not appropriate to just focus on one area of a child's development but that instead we need to consider how all areas of development are interlinked so that each one impacts on the other. In the context of young children this means that if we are talking about what they are doing with their bodies we must also consider the impact on their brain and vice versa. Therefore, this chapter explores the importance of considering movement in children's learning. The chapter begins by looking

DOI: 10.4324/9781003386728-4

at the environment that adults provide for children and how they can ensure that it is an environment supportive of effective interactions which are in turn supportive of children's physical and cognitive development. We focus on the importance of features in these environments that stimulate children's curiosity.

The second section of the chapter goes on to explore what kinds of knowledge it is important for adults who care for and look after young children to have. This might be knowledge that will enable them to recognise if a child is struggling in terms of their physical development. We signpost various sources of information that can help our understanding. At the same time, we remind ourselves that newspaper headlines and social media are not always the best sources of information and that it is important to consider critically what we read.

In the final section of the chapter, we explore in greater depth some of the children's behaviours that adults may observe whilst children are engaging in physical activity. We consider different ways that adults can successfully support children's physical development and learning. You will turn your attention to your own practice and consider how what you have learnt so far may change some of your own behaviours whilst caring for young children.

You are invited to consider the links between physical development and autonomy, recognising the important role that physical development plays in children learning to become independent and how this is important for their wellbeing. As you reflect on children's repetitive actions in physical development, you can consider how this links to what we know about schema. By the end of this chapter, we hope you will be able to confidently describe the holistic nature of children's development and also explain some of the impact a child's environment has on their holistic development. You should be able to identify the importance of practitioner, parental and carer knowledge in supporting young children's physical development, identify aspects of physical development in young children's everyday activity and discuss how physical development contributes to all areas of learning. Throughout the chapter we continue to reference the key wellbeing themes of communication, relationships, inclusion, partnership and trust.

This chapter is going to pose three key questions and then offer some suggestions of how we might answer them. These three questions are:

- How does physical development link to young children's holistic development and wellbeing?
- What do I need to know about children's movement, learning and wellbeing?
- What do I need to do to support young children's learning and wellbeing through movement?

How does physical development link to young children's holistic development and wellbeing?

Physical development is an important part of a child's holistic development but what do we actually mean in practice when we talk about a young child's holistic development? We often use this term to describe a way of seeing a child as a whole person whose areas of development intertwine and interact with each other. We can see what this looks like in practice by reading the description of Monique (9 months old) by Doherty and Hughes (2014, p. 26). They describe an everyday scenario of a baby at mealtime. At first glance it may look like the child is merely developing fine motor skills by learning to hold a cup; however, the authors encourage us to look more closely by indicating in brackets all the other learning that is taking place:

> Over the past few months, her mother and father have helped to feed her and encouraged her to hold the plastic cup on her high chair and guide it to Monique's lips. The cup sits in front of her as usual but one morning while waiting, she looks at it intently [perception] and moves a hand towards it. At first, she knocks the cup but then grasps it firmly and raises it off the plastic tray [physical]; 'Oooh' she gurgles [language] as her mother rushes over smiling and saying' 'What a clever girl. Well done Monique!' Monique beams back at her [social] and gurgles again.

Therefore, although there can be a tendency to think about some areas of learning and development, such as language or maths, as happening only in the brain and as solely intellectual pursuits, learning noticeably happens through physical interactions.

- Can you think of examples when you have seen different aspects of development in a child's simple action?
- You might like to think of a child doing something physical (jumping, climbing, gripping, drawing) and consider what other learning could have been taking place. Perhaps you have your own children where you have noticed this, or it could be children that you work with.
- You also might like to consider what the impact might have been if Monica had received a negative response from her mother, for example, if she had spilled her drink or made a mess.

Interacting with the environment

The environment provided for children to develop physically is all-important and need not be something that costs a lot of money. Not all children have access to a large garden, gymnastic clubs or forest schools. However, the knowledgeable adult can cheaply enhance any environment to provide as many opportunities as possible so that the environment becomes 'a third educator' (Strong-Wilson and Ellis, 2009); this is a phrase we use in Early Childhood Education and Care (ECEC) to describe how the environment is as important as both the child and the adult in a child's learning.

The skilled adult will look for a range of opportunities to support children in their physical development. Included in this will be space and resources. For example, they may push the furniture back to make a space to dance and then provide scarves or ribbons, picked up cheaply from a charity shop, to help the child extend their movements as they dance. They may look for other easily accessible resources within the environment to support the development of fine motor skills. For example, collections of plastic bottles with their corresponding lids are cheap, easily accessed in most homes and can keep children (aged 3–4 years) absorbed, building up their concentration as they try to match the correct lid to the bottle and tighten them. These adults will continually consider what already exists in the environment to enhance physical development.

A final important feature to provide in the environment are opportunities to stimulate a child's curiosity. Many people will recognise the need to put precious ornaments out of the child's way once they start crawling. The child moves towards them out of curiosity; they are the young scientist exploring their environment (Wray, 1999). Therefore, it is not a simple matter of moving precious or dangerous objects out of the way, we must think about what we are replacing them with. Elfer and Selleck (2022) emphasise the importance of touch to young children's learning. They cite the early years pioneer Susan Isaacs, who believed that asking a child not to touch was the same as asking them not to learn (Elfer and Selleck 2022, p. 136). Therefore, these removed ornaments and objects should be replaced with others safe for a child to move towards and explore, objects that will excite them and make them curious. Remember a moving child is a learning child.

This idea of moving, exploration and learning are brought together in the idea of heuristic play, which was a kind of play promoted by the seminal theorist Elinor Goldschmied. Goldschmied (1986) specifically introduced the idea of the treasure basket to support this kind of learning. Treasure baskets are collections of household objects often made from natural objects. They are safe and suitable for young babies especially to crawl towards, select an item and then use all their senses to explore that object. These everyday objects stimulate curiosity and therefore a child's movement. You will be able to read more about enhancing environments to enable physical play in Chapter 5.

Indoors or outdoors?

Imagine for a moment a group of young children engaged in physical activity. Think about what they are doing but, more importantly for this section, think about where they are. Did you place them in an outdoor environment? We imagine that you did because when we think about what young children can learn outdoors, we generally equate this space with physical activity.

It is not surprising that the outdoors is viewed as an optimal space for physical activity. Common sense thinking tells us that it is good for children to be in the fresh air, to 'puff and pant', to have the space they need to move at different speeds or throw and kick balls. Yet this type of common-sense thinking is not without issues that it is important to examine. These issues, highlighted by Kemp and Josephidou (2021) and Josephidou, Kemp and Durrant (2021), include:

- **The youngest children are excluded**: outdoors is seen as a place for those children already walking.
- **Learning indoors is privileged**: indoors is seen as a place to sit still and learn whilst outdoors is seen as somewhere to let off steam.
- **Access to the outdoors is not equal**: not all children have the same access to outdoor spaces; even spaces within early years settings differ greatly.

These issues are problematic for young children's holistic learning, development and wellbeing. This is because the outdoors is a perfect space for them as they grow and develop. Bento and Dias (2017) believe this is due to the 'open and constantly changing environment' (p. 157) that provides so many possibilities for all areas of development. We only have to consider the way that young children learn and 'their need to touch, taste, smell, look and manipulate with fingers and toes' (Elfer and Selleck, 2022, p. 136) to see that this is true. Think back for example to our consideration of the importance of all the senses in Chapter 2. The outdoors can offer so many multisensory opportunities; it is like one great treasure basket (McTavish, 2023).

Regardless of the fact that we would argue that physical development is for both indoors and outdoors, it is unfortunate that there is not equality of access for all children to the outdoor environment. This access can very much depend on where you live, what kind of setting you attend and the socio-economic status of your family. Provision in settings varies widely (Josephidou, Kemp and Durrant, 2021), with some settings providing free-flow between the indoors and the outdoors, whilst others have to navigate the layout of inappropriate buildings to let the children access an outdoor area.

To sum up this section, we would encourage you to remember that, although the outdoors is an important space for physical activity, it is important to not just equate this space with physical development. Not only does such thinking lead to a view of the indoors as a more sedentary area, but it also encourages the thinking that if the children can't get outside then they can't be physically active. Think for example about your experiences of rainy day playtimes in a school setting. It is better to not engage in what can be termed 'binary thinking' which divides indoors and outdoors into the kinds of activities that can be done there when we are thinking about young children. This type of thinking can lead to seeing barriers to both outdoors engagement and physical activity, instead of thinking more holistically about development and also about the learning spaces children need.

Spaces for physical development

In the last section, we thought about the indoor and outdoor space as environments for physical and holistic development, but we can add another layer to our discussion here. Try to think about all the indoor/outdoor spaces a young child might engage in. You might like to have a go at completing the table below.

How many different spaces did you manage to think of? You may have thought about the early years setting (both indoor and outdoor), the playground (outdoor) and the home environment (indoor and outdoor). It is easy to think about these spaces in quite a neutral, uncritical way in terms of their impact on children's physical and holistic development but there are certain factors it is important to consider. For example, if we return to the idea of inequality of access, some research, such as Weck (2019) suggests that middle-class parents can come to dominate certain playgrounds so that other

Table 4.1 Spaces for physical development

Spaces for physical development	
Indoors	*Outdoors*
E.g. Soft play area	E.g. Playground

parents feel judged, marginalised or not welcomed. The Natural England report (2019) also picked up on the idea that children and families living in less middle-class areas have a lack of access to green spaces.

And it is not just whether there are spaces available for physical development for young children; it also matters what the adults around them do in terms of making these spaces available. For example, several pieces of research have found that parents will assume that if their child is attending an early years setting, then they don't have to worry about finding opportunities for physical development. This is a worry if we note pieces of research like Carsley et al. (2017), who found that 'Recent studies suggest that the majority of time spent in daycare is sedentary' and that the almost 3000 children in their research (aged 1–5) had less outdoor play than those who didn't attend an early years setting. This suggests the importance of professional relationships with parents and working effectively with them to share the importance of physical development and also how they can support their children.

TIME TO REFLECT

Spend some time now reflecting on the environment you provide for young children in your care. This may be in a setting or it may be in the home environment. How do you ensure that you provide an environment that is the 'third educator'? An environment where children are supported to move and learn. The environment can and should offer multiple opportunities to enhance and encourage physical development. Look around the environment you provide for children and ask yourself how many opportunities are provided and how varied they are. Can children run, jump, crawl, dance, climb, roll? Can they manipulate objects? Can they make big movements and small movements, slow movements and quick movements? Can they feel exhilarated and a sense of accomplishment? We would argue an environment that offers all these possibilities is not only vital but needn't be expensive.

What do I need to know about young children's movement, learning and wellbeing?

In the last section we discussed how important the role of the environment is; in this section we are going to look more closely at parent or practitioner knowledge and think about why this is important knowledge to have, particularly if we consider issues of inclusion.

Noticing

Along with knowledge, the adult needs to be a noticer. Observation is a key part of early years pedagogy but we are not talking here about formal observations, just being attuned to the child and being able to 'listen' to what the child's physical movements, as part of their wider holistic development, are telling us. Norman (2022) explains the approach generally taken by practitioners to this 'listening' in the West:

> [It is a] . . . predominately . . . maturational development perspective (sequential approach and included areas of physical, intellectual language, emotions and social development (PILES) or social, physical, intellectual communication and emotional development (SPICE) in understanding and measuring abilities . . . [this means that] . . . Through signposting and plotting milestones parents and practitioners can examine development at an anticipated rate.
>
> (p. 73)

Sometimes practitioners and parents can be confused over the role they should be carrying out as they accompany young children's play and learning. Although it is important to interact with children to enhance learning and development, it is equally important to sometimes adopt a 'watching and waiting approach' (Bennett et al., 1997) so that we are not 'hijacking' their play and experiences (Fisher, 2016). Careful observation is a key skill for those working with young children and it is important to know what the learning needs of the child are and then how the environment could be enhanced to meet these. It is important that we continually stress the uniqueness of each child and how they will develop at their own pace;

however, careful observation may highlight areas that the practitioner or parent may be concerned about. For example, what if all your child's peers are already walking but your child shows no interest? What if the 4-year-old in your setting seems particularly clumsy? When is it important to get further information or advice?

There is a wealth of information to support parents and practitioners who want to find out if a child's physical development is anything to be concerned about. One useful resource is 'What to expect, when?' (4Children, 2015). This booklet focuses on all areas of development and is useful for anyone caring for children. Although it emphasises that each child will have their own unique journey of development, it signposts what you might observe at different ages. It also offers helpful examples of how adults can interact with children at these different ages. It will help you to decide whether you need to seek further help or advice, either from a medical or educational professional, if you have concerns about a child's holistic development.

Behind the headlines

In 2019, the World Health Organisation (WHO) updated some of their recommendations for physical activity for young children under the age of 5. Their report states that the guidelines are for all children 'irrespective of gender, cultural background or socio-economic status' (2019; viii). They also state that the guidelines are research-informed. These updated guidelines were then picked up and interpreted by the press in different ways. For example:

- 'No sedentary screen time for babies' (Roberts, 2019)
- 'Guidance recommends no screen time for under-twos' (Nursery World, 2019)
- 'Kids under two should never be allowed to watch ANY screens – or they'll get fat' (McDermott, 2019)

When we are surrounded by these kinds of headlines, it is easy to panic about how we are bringing our children up and what the best guidance is. We need to be able to look at the headlines critically and delve a bit deeper to know how they relate to the children in our care. For example, the recommendations made about screen time in the WHO report only make up a very small section; other issues it covers include physical activity, sedentary behaviour and sleep.

It's not easy to find advice on whether babies should be watching television, and for how long. The American Academy of Pediatrics recommend that the only type of digital media that children under 18 months should be engaging with is chatting by video calling. And the NHS suggests that television for under 2s should be limited to 30 minutes per day. These are all useful sources of information to inform our practice.

Links to practice

Aisha is worried because the mums at her group have been talking about how harmful technology can be for young children. They talk about scary newspaper headlines about children who are sitting still for too long. She wonders if she should take the iPad off her son, who is 3 years old. What advice would you give her?

Comment

Some students thought about the question above and these are some of their responses:

> *Rather than talking too much about the negative aspects of too much screen time I would highlight the amazing benefits of spending one-to-one time with your child and providing opportunities for first hand experiences for their enjoyment, their learning, relationship building and their general wellbeing.*

I would advise Aisha to keep a record of how long her son is on his iPad everyday. If she finds that her son is spending too long on it each day, I would help her come up with things that would help to increase her son's physical activity levels. This could include letting her son play in the garden or park. Aisha could also think about when her son is on his iPad. If he is on the iPad before his bedtime, I would suggest that Aisha ensures that he plays on the iPad earlier in the day so that his sleep is less likely to be interrupted. If her son is on his iPad for a short time each day, then I would advise Aisha to not be too concerned about this. The reality is that young children will have to learn to use technology such as iPads. They probably have them in some nurseries now and they will certainly need digital skills in preparation for starting school. I would therefore advise Aisha that it is important that her son knows how to use digital technology such as iPads, so I would advise against removing his use of the iPad completely. There may also be educational games her son could play on the iPad.

As with anything in life, everything in moderation. The iPad is part of modern day life, before that it was TV and before that it was Elvis on the radio. Children need guidance. I love watching something on tv or the iPad and then applying what we watched to real life. For example: the reluctant walker who forgets about that as they transform into Dora the Explorer....or the child who doesn't want to share recollecting Peppa Pig's story. It has its place...

TIME TO REFLECT

In this section we have considered the importance of supportive knowledgeable adults if we want to encourage healthy physical development in young children. We have also looked at different ways parents, carers and practitioners can be supportive. It would be a good point to stop and reflect now on what you have learnt so far. Have a go at responding to the following questions:

* When you are working with or looking after young children, what are you looking for in terms of their physical development?
* Think about a newspaper headline you have seen recently that has made you question what you are doing or should be doing.
* Is it important to change your practice in light of this headline – or do you need to do a bit more research?
* What is one thing you could change about your practice given what you have read in this chapter so far?

What do I need to do to support young children's learning and wellbeing through movement?

In the last section we focused on what the adult caring for young children needs to *know* regarding their physical development. You will already be aware that the relationship between adult and child is key, so it will now be appropriate to focus much more on adult behaviours in relation to child behaviours i.e., what the adult should *do*. By carefully watching children at play, the adult can look for ways to enhance every opportunity of movement and learning.

Supportive adults

What should the supportive adult be doing to encourage young children in their physical development? We have discussed how adults can resource the environment but what things should they be doing when they interact with the children to encourage physical activity? We know that adult–child interactions are very important in play as outlined by Vygotsky (Gupta, 2009). Vygotsky was a famous Russian psychologist whose work has had a lot of impact on how we engage with young children, particularly in educational settings. A key phrase of his translates into English as the 'More Knowledgeable Other' (MKO); this describes the adult who supports a child in their play to ensure that learning and development takes place. The MKO could be defined as one who supports a child to work within their Zone of Proximal Development (ZPD), either by their questions, assertions or actions. Bennett et al. (1997, p. 12) describe the ZPD as 'the difference between the actual and potential development' of a child. In this context it is how the adult accompanies physical play and communicates with the child that can support them in achieving this potential. Let's look at an example in practice of this kind of support. An adult watches a child jumping and says:

- How can you make yourself jump higher? (question)
- If you use your arms and bend your knees you can jump higher! (assertion)
- Look at me! (action: the adult models how to jump higher)

To understand better how and when to use questions, assertions and modelling, the adult will be observing closely the child at physical play, but what should they be looking for, especially if we think about different age groups? If we think about the youngest children, for example, such as babies and toddlers, we are looking for seemingly simple actions, although complex to them, such as signs that they are:

- grasping and releasing objects
- mouthing objects
- using hand–eye co-ordination
- pointing
- self-feeding – and being messy in the process!

There are in fact specific milestones we can look for in that first year.

Milestones from birth to 14 months

The supportive adult needs to consider not just the children's behaviours but also their own. For example, are they ensuring that they are engaging in warm, encouraging interactions? Josephidou and Kemp (2022) found that practitioners talked about practices of 'meerkating' when looking after children engaged in physical play, i.e., they stood watching ready to rush over if needed. They

Table 4.2 Physical development milestones from birth to 14 months.

Age	Milestone
6 weeks	Hold head upright whilst in a prone position
2 months	Roll from back onto side
3 months	Reach for objects
5–7 months	Sit without support
9–14 months	Stand without support
8–12 months	Walk with support
12 months	Use of pincer grasp
12–14 months	Walk alone

Adapted from Keenan and Evans (2009, p. 99)

perhaps adopt a supervisory role because they are worried about the children getting hurt. This is so easy to do, but can lead to children feeling anxious about physical activity if their physical play is accompanied by of exclamations of 'Look out! Be careful! Slow down'. You will read more about supporting rough and tumble and risky play in Chapter 5.

Supporting children to become independent

As children become independent walkers, their physical development is closely aligned with them wanting autonomy to make their own choices, interact with others and imitate cultural practices. Think for example about children playing in a sand and water tray in a setting. Of course, they will be engaging in early scientific and mathematical thinking, they will be developing language as they interact with others – but what about their physical development? Try to list all the physical movements they may be making, both gross and fine. Did you come up with a long list to include:

- gripping
- pushing
- twisting
- lifting
- reaching
- pulling
- placing
- poking
- tracing
- patting
- hitting...?

You probably thought of many others. It is interesting to note physical development happening indoors because, as we have already noted, often it is the outdoors that is equated with physical activity, with indoors restricted to fine motor skills of mark-making, cutting and small construction. However, there are many opportunities for children to engage in gross motor skills indoors if an enabling environment is provided.

Supporting children and repetitive actions

We cannot discuss movement and learning in young children without acknowledging the importance of **schema** in their holistic development. Schema can be defined as a 'framework that places concepts, objects, or experiences into categories' (Levine and Munsch, 2011, p. 233). As children make sense of their world, including new concepts, objects and experiences, they develop schema and act out their understanding through their movements. For instance, May (2011) gives the example of a child who is exploring the concept of circles; they spend time making circular movements such as stirring a toy pan, painting round shapes or dancing until they are dizzy (p.21). Cathy Nutbrown, a professor of Early Childhood at Sheffield University, has worked with the BBC to create a TV programme, *Twirlywoos*, for young children, which acknowledges and incorporates their learning and development need for schema.

Links to practice

Paul is worried that his 2-year-old son, Dylan, has suddenly begun to throw things. He came home from nursery upset because he was told off for throwing bricks. Paul is concerned he will get a reputation as a 'naughty' boy. One of the other dads, who had watched Nutbrown's programme and had been interested to find out a bit more, suggests that Dylan may have a trajectory schema (i.e., he may be exploring ideas around movement and direction). Paul is able to do some research on the internet about how best to help his son explore these concepts in a safe way. He also prints off some resources to take into the nursery and after talking about his concerns and thoughts with Dylan's key person, she sets up some outdoor games such as throwing beanbags into buckets. Dylan can now carry on throwing and exploring his trajectory schema but now he doesn't have to worry about getting it wrong, hurting anyone or being reprimanded. Some of the other children enjoy joining in with exploring throwing also.

As you care for young children, have you noticed any schema developing? Sometimes they can be problematic, as Paul and the nursery found out!

Think about young children you work with or care for and some of their movement behaviours that could be schema. How could you best support them? And how do you partner with parents to support these repetitive behaviours. Table 4.3 below gives you an idea of some of the schema you may have noticed:

Table 4.3 Schema you may notice in young children

Schema	Physical actions you may observe	Activities you can provide
Trajectory	Throwing Climbing Jumping in puddles	Chasing bubbles Playing with scarves in the wind Throwing balls
Transporting	Moving resources Carrying many items Holding baskets and containers	Gathering twigs, fir cones, sticks and leaves Transporting using buckets, boxes, bags, baskets and wheeled toys
Enclosing	Constructing fences and barricades	Playing hide and seek Making dens
Rotational	Turning taps on and off Winding and unwinding string Twirling and twisting their body Spinning around on the spot Rolling down a hill	Throwing, catching and kicking balls Playing on roundabouts Playing with hoops.
Enveloping	Covering and hiding objects Dressing up Filling and emptying bags and containers	Wrapping presents Filling containers Dressing up Wrapping teddies in blankets
Connecting	Joining objects together Tying string Gluing and sticking	Connecting train tracks Threading Junk modelling
Orientation	Turning objects and themselves upside down	Climbing Rolling Rough and tumble

Adapted from Education Scotland (n.d.)

Supporting children in appropriate risk-taking

Another key term associated with physical opportunities for young children is 'risk taking'. Positive risk-taking is an important part of children's lives; it develops their confidence, their thinking skills, their creative skills, their problem-solving skills and is vital for their wellbeing. But what does this term actually mean? Let's look at some definitions from those who have carried out research with young children in this area:

- Little et al. (2011, p. 115) describe it as 'opportunities for challenge, testing limits, exploring boundaries and learning about injury-risk'.
- Stephenson (2003) described it as 'attempting something never done before, feeling on the borderline of "out of control" often because of height or speed, and overcoming fear' (p. 36).
- Greenfield (2004) said 4-year-old children talked about 'risk, speed, excitement, thrills, uncertainty and challenge' (p. 4).

However, both parents and practitioners can worry about risk-taking, however appropriate it may be. This is problematic because, unsurprisingly, parents who worry about risk have children who are much less confident in engaging in managed risk in their physical activity. Murray and Williams (2020) suggest that there is work to be done in supporting parental understandings of challenge in outdoor physical activity and developing trust between both setting and parent and adult and child, as parents in their research sample 'who rated outdoor . . . [physical activity] . . . scenarios as more risky tended to have children who exhibited more risk aversion'.

In this section we have looked at how the adult can best engage with children in terms of physical development. We have noted how they can support children in becoming independent by recognising the link between physical development and autonomy, we have considered schematic behaviours you could look out for, and we have reminded ourselves of the importance of appropriate risk taking in movement and learning. You will be able to read more about how appropriate risk-taking in physical activity relates to play in Chapter 5.

Concluding thoughts

In this chapter, we have considered how children physically interact with their environment to develop holistically. We have also seen how important physical development is for all other areas of development and for children's wellbeing when they are learning and developing. Therefore, as those who work with or care for young children, it is vital that we have a good under-standing of children's developmental needs and behaviours. Sometimes these behaviours can present in such a way that adults find them difficult to deal with, such as schema; it is important that we can recognise when children are demonstrating learning and what the role of the adult should be. You may have been thinking about how you can apply what you have learnt in this chapter. Have a look at the top tips below and think about how you might include them in your care of young children.

Top tips

- **Be active yourself**: put the radio on and dance around the room. Your child will copy you.
- **Be a collector**: make a collection of things that will enhance your child's physical development. You might like to make a treasure basket or box. Have a look at what is already in the environment without going out and spending money.
- **Ask questions**: when you observe your child moving try to ask ques-tions which will enhance their movements. You might find you do this without thinking.
- **Be an encourager**: use language which encourages children to extend themselves in physical movement.
- **Allow choice**: consider how you encourage autonomy and choice as your child becomes more independent.
- **Be a problem solver**: if you notice some movement behaviours which are problematic, such as throwing, see if you can introduce activities where children can act out their ideas safely.

Key terms

Pedagogies	Ways the adult chooses to teach and support the young child in their learning and development.
Cognitive development	How young children learn to think, explore, work things out and remember.
Autonomy	How a young child grows in independence.
Schema	A framework young children develop to make sense of the world.
Holistic development	How all areas of a child's development intertwine and interact with each other.
Perception	How children use their senses to collect information about what they see around them.
Enhance	Improve the opportunities for young children (here in the environment).
Multisensory	When learning provides the opportunity for children to use lots of different senses.
Freeflow	When children make their own choices about where to play.
Sedentary	When children spend a lot of time sitting down.

In the next chapter, you will build on the learning from this week to focus specifically on the links between movement, play and learning. We will explore different kinds of play and how they support physical development. In addition, we will consider how the parent or practitioner can plan for play, including planning an environment which supports children's physical development and yet, at the same time, does not cost a lot of money to set up.

 Further reading

Grimmer, T. (2017) *Observing and Developing Schematic Behaviour in Young Children*. London: Jessica Kingsley.

Hughes, A. (2015) *Developing Play for the Under 3s: The Treasure Basket and Heuristic Play* (3rd edn). Abingdon: Routledge.

O'Connor, A. and Daly, A. (2016) *Understanding Physical Development in the Early Years*. Abingdon: Routledge.

References

Bennett, N., Wood, L. and Rogers, S. (1997) *Teaching through Play: Teachers' Thinking and Classroom Practice*. Buckingham: OUP.

Bento, G. and Dias, G. (2017) 'The importance of outdoor play for young children's healthy development', *Porto Biomedical Journal*, 2(5), pp. 157–160. doi:10.1016/j.pbj.2017.03.003

Bilton, H. (2004) 'Movement as a vehicle for learning', in Miller, L. and Devereux, J. (eds) *Supporting Children's Learning in the Early Years*. London: David Fulton.

Carsley, S., L.Y. Liang, Y., Chen, P. Parkin, J., Maguire, C.S., Birken, (2017) on behalf of the TARGet Kids! Collaboration, 'The impact of daycare attendance on outdoor free play in young children, *Journal of Public Health*, 39(1), March, pp. 145–152. Available at: https://doi-org.libezproxy.open.ac.uk/10.1093/pubmed/fdw006

Doherty and Hughes (2014) *Child Development: Theory and Practice 0–11*. Harlow: Pearson Longman.

Education Scotland (n.d.) *Schemas: Learning through Play*. Available at: https://education.gov.scot/parentzone/Documents/nih058-Parentzone-Booklet.pdf

Elfer, P. and Selleck, D. (2022). 'Elinor Goldschmied', in Palmer, A. and Read, J. (eds) *British Froebelian Women from the Mid-Nineteenth to the Twenty-First Century*. Abingdon: Routledge.

Fisher, J. (2016). *Interacting or Interfering? Improving Interactions in the Early Years*. Maidenhead: Open University Press.

Fletcher, R., St. George, J. and Freeman, F. (2013) 'Rough and tumble play quality: Theoretical foundations for a new measure of father–child interaction, *Early Child Development and Care*, 183(6), pp. 746–759.

4Children (2015) *What to Expect, When?* Available at https://www.eyalliance.org.uk/sites/default/files/what_to_expect_when._a_parents_guide.pdf

Goldschmied, E. (1986) *Infants at Work: Babies of 6 to 9 Months Exploring Everyday Objects*. DVD/video. London: Jessica Kingsley.

Greenfield, C. (2004) '"Can run, play on bikes, jump the zoom slide, and play on the swings": Exploring the value of outdoor play, *Australian Journal of Early Childhood*, 29(2), pp. 1–5.

Gupta, A. (2009) 'Vygotskian perspectives on using dramatic play to enhance children's development and balance creativity with structure in the early childhood classroom', *Early Child Development and Care*, 179(8), pp. 1041–1054.

Josephidou, J. and Kemp, N. (2022) 'A life 'in and with nature?' Developing nature engaging and nature enhancing pedagogies for babies and toddlers', *Global Education Review*, 9 (2), pp. 5–22.

Josephidou, J., Kemp, N. and Durrant, I. (2021) 'Outdoor provision for babies and toddlers: Exploring the practice/policy/research nexus in English ECEC settings', *European Early Childhood Education Research Journal*, 29(6).

Keenan, T. and Evans, S. (2009) *An Introduction to Child Development*. London: Sage.

Kemp, N. and Josephidou, J. (2021) 'Babies and toddlers outdoors: A narrative review of the literature on provision for under twos in ECEC settings', *Early Years*, doi: 10.1080/09575146.2021.1915962

Levine, L.E. and Munsch, J. (2011) *Child Development: An Active Learning Approach*. London: Sage.

Little, H., Wyver, S. and Gibson, F. (2011) 'The influence of play context and adult attitudes on young children's physical risk-taking during outdoor play', *European Early Childhood Education Research Journal*, 19(1), pp. 113–131.

May, P. (2011) *Child Development in Practice*. Abingdon: Routledge.

McDermott, N. (2019) 'SWITCH OFF Kids under two should never be allowed to watch ANY screens – or they'll get fat, WHO warns', *Sun*. Available at: https://www.thesun.co.uk/news/8929504/kids-under-two-no-tv-screens-obesity-who/

McTavish, A. (2023) *Treasure Baskets and Heuristic Play*. Available at: https://early-education.org.uk/treasure-baskets-and-heuristic-play/

Murray, E.J. and Hrusa Williams, P. (2020) 'Risk-tasking and assessment. in toddlers during nature play: The role of family and play context,

Journal of Adventure Education and Outdoor Learning, 20(3), pp. 259–273.

Natural England (2019). Monitor of Engagement with the Natural Environment. The national survey on people and the natural environment. Children and Young People report. Available at: https://assets.publishing.service.gov.uk/government/uploads/system /uploads/attachment_data/file/828838/Monitor_of_Engagement_ with_the_Natural_Environment__MENE__Childrens_Report_2018 -2019_rev.pdf

NHS (2021) *Baby and toddler play ideas*. Available at: https://www.nhs .uk/conditions/pregnancy-and-baby/play-ideas-and-reading/

Norman, A. (2022) *Historical Perspectives on Infant Care and Development*. London: Bloomsbury.

Nursery World (2019) 'Guidance recommends no screen time for under-twos', *Nursery World*. Available at: https://www.nurseryworld.co .uk/news/article/guidance-recommends-no-screen-time-for-under -twos

Roberts, M. (2019) 'No sedentary screen time for babies, WHO says', BBC. Available at: https://www.bbc.co.uk/news/health-48021224

Stephenson, A. (2003) 'Physical risk-taking: Dangerous or endangered?' *Early Years*, 23(1), pp. 35–43.

Strong-Wilson, T. and Ellis, J. (2009) Children and place: Reggio Emilia's environment as third teacher, *Theory into Practice*, 46(1), pp. 40–47.

Weck, S. (2019) '"Together apart" or "apart together"? – middle-class. parents' choice of playgrounds and playground interactions in socially diverse neighbourhoods', *Social & Cultural Geography*, 20(5), pp. 710–729, doi:10.1080/146493 65.2017.1373302

WHO (2019) *To Grow up Healthy, Children Need to Sit Less and Play More*. Available at: https://www.who.int/news/item/24-04-2019-to -grow-up-healthy-children-need-to-sit-less-and-play-more

Wray, D. (1999) 'Teaching literacy: The foundations of good practice', *Education 3–13*, 27(1), pp. 53–59.

Play and physical development in early childhood

Lucy Rodriguez Leon

Introduction

The previous chapters have showcased just how important it is for babies and young children to have a wide range of opportunities to develop gross motor (whole body) and fine motor (manipulative) movement skills, and to stimulate vestibular and proprioceptive senses through movement. Learning to move is also vital for children's wellbeing; it opens up new play and exploration opportunities for babies. Becoming independently mobile increases opportunities to make decisions and be autonomous. Mobility helps children to initiate social interactions with parents, family or peers, and being mobile and active enables young children to interact with their environment in increasingly complex ways.

This chapter explores the crucial role of play in children's physical and holistic development, and their wellbeing. Firstly, you will consider the concept of play, and how the term can refer to a wide range of different activities. You will explore how different environments afford different opportunities for children to move and develop physical skills. You will think about the pros and cons of risky play, and rough and tumble play, how these are important for children's development, but must be closely monitored. Finally, the chapter will discuss how everyday resources and materials, public spaces and early years environments can extend possibilities for physical play without the need for expensive equipment or classes.

DOI: 10.4324/9781003386728-5

Understanding the role of play in children's development and learning

Babies and young children have an innate desire to play. In contemporary Western cultures, it is generally accepted that young children learn through play. In fact, the United Nations Convention on the Right of the Child UNCRC (UNICEF, 1989) states play is a fundamental right for children; this is a view that is echoed in the early years curricula of many countries.

However, 'play' is a very broad term that can refer to a wide variety of different activities. Parents, practitioners, policymakers, researchers and children might all have very different ideas about what play is. In fact, it can be quite difficult to come up with a definition of play that aligns with everyone's perspectives and that covers play in all is different forms. The Charter for Play, by the organisation 'Play England' describes play as, 'what children and young people do when they follow their own ideas and interests, in their own way, and for their own reasons' (Play England, 2020). In many respects we agree with this definition, however, in this chapter we take a very broad view of play and acknowledge that adult-led activity can also be very playful and fun. It is also important to acknowledge that the ways children play differs between cultures and that different places and environments enable different sorts of play opportunities (Fleer, 2021). For example, young children in rural areas may have very different play spaces to children living in densely populated urban areas.

If you think back and reflect on your own early childhood play experiences, you might recall playing in the streets and communal spaces in your neighbourhood, or perhaps you grew up in a community where the streets were too busy for children to play. Maybe you were taken to parks and playgrounds to play, or maybe you had access to woodland. Outdoors, your play might have involved balls, skipping ropes, bikes or scooters, for example, or maybe you made use of natural resources such as sticks, rocks and mud. At times, your play might not have needed any resources or toys, particularly if you were playing with friends or siblings. Playing indoors might have involved construction toys, board games, imaginary play, cardboard boxes, dolls or soft toys, and so forth, or you might have played with a games console. Therefore, it is clear that play can include a wide range of activities;

Table 5.1 Hughes taxonomy of play types

Symbolic play	Play in which children use objects and actions to represent something else, for example, using a bowl as a steering wheel as they pretend to drive.
Rough and tumble play	Energetic play that involves close physical contact, such as play wrestling and tickling.
Socio-dramatic play	Re-enactment of real or plausible everyday experiences, such as playing at cooking, or being mummy or daddy.
Social play	Play that involves agreed rules or criteria to participate, such as some ball games, or 'stuck in the mud'.
Creative play	Play that involves designing, exploring, and testing new ideas, and that allows novel responses and mediums of self-expression, for example, making art, music or dance.
Communication play	Play that primarily involves words, gestures, rhymes, singing, mime and so forth, such as clapping games.
Dramatic play	Enactments of events that are outside of the child's own personal experience, such as acting out the events in a video game or cartoon.
Locomotor play	Play that is primarily about movement for its own sake, such as using a climbing frame or slide.
Deep play	Play that is adventurous and associated with a degree of risk. It often involves conquering fear, such as walking along a wall, or jumping from a height.
Exploratory play	Play that involves finding out information or discovering the properties of an object. For example, water play with sieves and funnels.
Fantasy play	Play that involves make-believe worlds, creating scenarios and scenes that are not plausible, such as being fairies or knights on horseback.
Imaginative play	Play that involves pretence and 'what if' thinking; this play is not constrained by reality. It might involve pretend interactions with an imaginary friend or pet.
Mastery play	Play that involves control over physical elements, such as building sandcastles or block towers.

Object play	Play that involves manipulating and exploring objects, such as babies mouthing a rattle, or shaking a bunch of keys.
Role play	Play that imitates ways of being and ways of doing things in play environments, such as cooking, or being the bus driver.
Recapitulative play	There is some controversy surrounding whether this is a 'type' of play. However, it is described as play that involves exploring history, ancestry or human rituals and practices.

play specialist Bob Hughes studied children's activity in different contexts and identified 16 different types of play, in what is known as the 'taxonomy of play' (Hughes, 2002).

Hughes' (2002) taxonomy of play is helpful to illustrate how play involves many diverse activities; however, young children's activity often involves multiple types of play at once, or it may seamlessly flow from one type of play to another.

You will see from the taxonomy of play that most play types involve some fine or gross motor skills, but not all types of play involve vigorous physical activity. However, whilst playing, children often repeat actions purely for pleasure, such as swinging, spinning, jumping, pushing / pulling, digging, pouring (water), or making marks, for example, and in doing so, they develop control or mastery of the action and stimulate their proprioceptive and vestibular senses. Therefore, children need opportunities to engage in many different sorts of play to promote physical development and to ensure they get the recommended levels of physical activity.

CASE STUDY

Aaliyah and Kyra

On arriving at playgroup, 2-year-olds Kyra and Aaliyah head for the outdoor sandpit and go straight to the large plastic box filled with resources, such as, old pans, spoons, ladles, buckets, spades, and so forth. Rather than selecting the items they want, Aaliyah grasps the handle on one side of the box, saying to Kyra, 'get it, get it', nodding towards the handle on the other side. With some effort, together they lift the box and empty the entire contents into the sand. They inspect the pile of items for a moment; Kyra selects a saucepan and a large spoon and sits down and begins filling the pan with sand. After every few spoonfuls, she stirs the contents, scraping the spoon around the metal edge with some force.

Meanwhile, Aaliyah selects a horse-shaped jelly mould, and uses her hands to fill it with sand, which she presses down firmly. She picks up the mould and carefully manoeuvres it with her hands, to enable her to turn it over. Once flipped, she pats the top and lifts the mould up revealing her (almost) horse-shaped sand sculpture. She proudly exclaims, 'daa-daah', grinning at Kyra.

Kyra smiles back and holds her pan out toward Aaliyah, saying 'pagetti, yeah, pagetti' (spaghetti) in a questioning tone. Aaliyah looks at the sand in the pan and laughs, then rolls back to lie in the sand, moving her arms and legs in and out, 'me doing snow angel' she says. Kyra drops her pan and copies; they both shriek with laughter.

The case study illustrates how, in this short episode, these 2-year-olds engaged in role play, mastery play, object play, exploratory play and locomotor play, whilst using a wide range of fine and gross motor skills. It demonstrates that play is fundamental to young children's development and well-being; many books have been written on the complexities and importance of play in early childhood. However, the next section focuses specifically on physically active play, how it promotes children's holistic development, and the role of adults in modelling and supporting physically active play.

 TIME TO REFLECT

Take a moment to recall a recent play scenario that was initiated by children in your care (rather than play you directed). Revisit the scenario in your mind's eye and think about the different sorts of play involved. Did the different sorts of play merge together, or did the play progress in such a way that it flowed from one type of play to another? If multiple children were involved, were they engaged together in the same type of play, or were children playing alongside each other, but engaged in different play types? Now consider the different types of movement involved; was it vigorous physically active play that left children out of breath? Did it involve exerting some force to push or lift heavy resources? Or did it require the careful manipulation of small pieces or small movements?

Promoting learning, development and well-being through physical play

Chapter 3 explored how fundamental movement skills provide the building blocks of children's physical literacy. However, movement skills do not develop in isolation; personal, social and emotional development, movement and coordination, communication and language, and creativity and curiosity are all interconnected, and together, lay the foundations for all areas of learning. It is said that children think with their bodies and their minds (Mountain, 2017); physically active play is not only a vehicle for physical development and exercise, but it also promotes and enhances many different areas of development. This section will explore some of these key aspects in turn.

Curiosity and creativity

Babies are curious, they pay attention to what is going on around them and they often respond to stimuli in their unique and creative ways. For example, they may turn toward the direction of a sound to see what's happening, and they might move their arms and legs, and make vocal sounds in response. Once babies are able to grasp an object, such as a rattle or feeding spoon, they will explore it with all their senses. They will examine it closely, bang and shake it, and mouth it to explore its texture, smell and taste, and how it sounds and looks. Young children's curiosity and creativity are most evident when they can play and move freely in a safe environment with stimulating, open-ended resources. This enables children to follow their own interests, to explore and investigate, to create their own imaginary worlds and to respond to various stimuli in their own ways (McConnon, 2016). This sort of free play often involves problem-solving, whether it's working out how construction toys fit together, or discovering how to navigate a scooter through a small gap, for example. By figuring out solutions to these challenges, children develop confidence and become more curious about how things work.

Personal, social and emotional development

From the moment they are born, babies begin to forge relationships with their parents, carers and other familiar people. They form close attachments through touch, smell, gaze, sound and so forth. As babies become mobile, opportunities to move and play allow them to widen their social relationships. Physically active play provides a channel through which friendships can be built and nurtured. When children play together, they interpret each other's body language, negotiate, take turns and coordinate their movement to progress the play. Finding common interests in play helps children to form bonds and trust in one another; they develop empathy and start to understand how their actions affect others. So, we can see that movement, play and wellbeing are closely linked.

In addition to the social value, physical play provides many opportunities for young children to challenge themselves and push the boundaries of their capabilities. Developing the coordination and movement skills to kick or throw a ball, to climb up a ladder, or to make a sandcastle takes practice and repetition. In this sort of play, children often experience failure before they succeed. However, in play, and with the encouragement of supportive adults and peers, children will repeat the activity many times until they achieve their goal and master the movement and skills required. Physical play can therefore build children's perseverance, resilience and confidence. It can also build a sense of empowerment; as children interact with others and the environment in play, they come to understand their own self-efficacy; that is, they begin to understand that they have an impact and can influence situations in which they participate (Canning, 2020).

Communication and language

Movement is our first and enduring language

(White, 2015: p. 77)

Long before infants learn to pronounce recognisable words, they express themselves and communicate through movement, actions, gestures and facial expression. In fact, throughout life, the ways in which we communicate and express ourselves are multimodal; even when we do master verbal language, we continue to use body language and vocal intonation to enhance the meaning of the words we speak (Kress, 2009).

At around 10–13 months, babies begin to use physical gestures for intentional communication, such as pointing with the index finger. Sometimes, pointing is a request for a toy or other item that the child cannot reach independently. However, the purpose of pointing can also be to draw another person's attention to something (a scene, object, image, animal or someone) they find interesting – in essence, pointing is about sharing an experience (Boundy et al., 2015). Pointing takes a degree of fine motor control, and this gesture, and other communicative gestures, develop when babies and young children have opportunities to interact with others, to move, to play and to explore the world around them.

As they grow and develop, children's physical play is often accompanied by verbal language, whether that be directed at others or simply self-expression; for example, the child at the top of the slide might shout, 'ready, steady, go', before launching themselves down the slide. During physical play with adults or peers, children learn the meaning of specific vocabulary associated with movement, space and shape (White, 2015). For example, they learn words to describe space and position (e.g., up, down, over, above), speed, time and distance (e.g., slow, fast, short, long), and sequence (e.g., before, after, first, then). Children use this vocabulary to communicate their plans and actions in physical activity; however, they are not just words, they are also concepts, which enable children to organise their thinking and understandings of the world.

CASE STUDY

Den-making

At an after-school club in Wales, den-making has been a popular activity over the summer. In the outdoor area, there is a selection of resources, including large wooden blocks, metal A-frames, poles and some blankets are available for children to use as they wish. The 4–6-year-olds have about half an hour before the older children arrive at the club, so five young children waste no time in getting to work on their den.

One child drags the large A-frame away from the wall, pulling hard, but not getting very far. Two others come over to help, and when they've moved it a few meters, one shouts, 'yeah, here'. Together, they bring large wooden blocks placing them haphazardly around the A-frame. They begin using them as stepping stones, leaping from one block to the other before going to retrieve another. When they have gathered all the blocks, they begin stacking them, two or three high around the A-frame. They negotiate the positioning of blocks, using phrases including, 'no, that's too close', 'further back', 'make it higher'. One child brings a folded blanket and tries to open it by shaking it vigorously; others come to help, and together they pull the blanket over the A-frame; one of the children shouts, 'yeah, we did it'. They begin to crawl under the covered A-frame with speed, then jump between the block stepping stones round the A-frame, making their own obstacle course. With no verbal coordination, they all follow the same route, traveling in the same direction. They move as fast as they can, shrieking and laughing with delight.

The case study above describes a very typical play event at an after-school club. Without any conscious effort, the children are engaged in vigorous physical activity, developing gross motor skills and coordination, and developing their vestibular and proprioceptive senses. There seemed to be a sense of camaraderie; the five children all cooperated, working together and taking turns seemed to be a natural part of the play. In fact, they required very little verbal communication to coordinate their movements. During this short play episode, the children challenged themselves and persevered, and it seems safe to say that the play fostered their self-esteem and sense of self-efficacy; these sorts of experiences are key to children's wellbeing.

The case study illustrates how physically active play has great value for children's holistic development, not just their physical development and health. However, adults can sometimes get a little nervous when children's physical play becomes a little risky or gets too boisterous.

Risky play and rough and tumble play

All adults who care for children have a responsibility to keep them safe and protect them from harm; risk must always be assessed in relation to a child's stage of development.

However, some early childhood scholars in the UK and internationally suggest that parental and societal concerns over children's safety have grown significantly in a generation; we have become a risk-averse society. This has limited children's opportunities to participate in vigorous physical activity and challenging play, especially in outdoor spaces (e.g., Little, 2017; Sandseter, Sando and Kleppe, 2021; Solly, 2015). Research in the Early Childhood Education and Care (ECEC) sectors in both the UK and Australia has found that many practitioners recognise the value and broad learning potential of risky play, yet feel constrained by regulation and the accountability that goes with caring for other people's children (Little, 2016).

The previous chapter presented three definitions of 'risky play', which together suggested that risk involves some sort of hazard, perceived danger, and potential for physical injury, for example, height, speed or uncertainty. Supervising young children whilst they engage in risky play can cause a degree of anxiety for parents or practitioners, and there may be a tendency to 'err on the side of caution'. However, as Lindon (2011) points out, it is important that we build children's confidence, not their anxieties, and be mindful not to create a culture of fear about physical play.

Embracing risky play does not mean allowing children to engage in dangerous activity, such as unknowingly entering deep or fast flowing water, or venturing onto the ice on a frozen pond (Tremblay et al., 2015). During appropriate risky play, children are aware of their competence, they recognise the risk, evaluate the situation and decide on a course of action. Risky play enables children test their own limitations and capabilities; it allows children to step a little way out of their comfort zone. The factors determining what is 'risk' in play are very individual; what is risky for one 3-year-old might be very safe and easy for another. They may try something new, they might climb a little higher than before, jump off a higher step, go faster, try the slide backwards or ride a bike for the first time, for example. These might all be very small steps in children's physical development; however, they could result in giant leaps in their confidence and sense of achievement.

Young children may need the support of an adult when they first attempt an activity in which they perceive risk, and some children may need the gentle encouragement of a sensitive and supportive adult to attempt a new physical challenge for the first time. However, it is important that children are able to take risks in a supervised play environment, to develop their ability to perceive, assess and manage risk and dangers for themselves. In physically active play, risk and challenge go hand-in-hand. Challenge refers to a situation in which a child can extend their own abilities and skills, or overcome fears (Solly, 2015). All children need appropriate opportunities to experience both risk and challenge in their play; in fact, many children seem attracted to challenge and actively seek it out.

Another type of play that can cause some anxiety for parents and practitioners is rough and tumble play. Babies seek close physical contact with the parents and carers, and they also enjoy being gently rocked, or softly tickled. As they grow older, many young children (but not all) enjoy vigorous and physical play with others that involves play wrestling, chasing, catching, falling on purpose, lifting and swinging each other, or rolling on the ground, for example. This type of play is often known as 'rough and tumble'. It is thought to be an 'evolutionary' type of play that is observed not only in human children, but also in the young of many species of mammals.

Rough and tumble play involves high levels of physical exertion and opportunity to develop motor skills. When familiar, sensitive adults engage in rough and tumble with children, they can usually 'read' their body language and adapt the play accordingly. However, parents and practitioners are sometimes concerned by rough and tumble between children as it can resemble fighting and aggression. Indeed, research has shown that rough and tumble play and chasing games are the most likely types of play to be limited or prohibited by teachers (Storli and Sandseter, 2015).

However, in children's activity, there are clear distinctions between what is play and what is aggression. Despite the appearance of fighting, rough and tumble play can build children's social competencies (Storli and Sandseter, 2015). Studies of rough and tumble play have shown that children often engage in peer support, fair-play and collaboration, and they negotiate and agree rules (Jarvis, 2007). Facial expression and vocalisations are key signs that rough and tumble wrestling is not aggressive or real fighting – it is often accompanied by smiling and laughing, participants take part equally, or they happily swap roles. Play fighting is often exaggerated and simulated, and usually takes place between close friends or siblings. During rough and tumble play, children choose to stay in the play situation, and they demonstrate self-control (Storli and Sandseter, 2015). It is a type of play that can provide valuable opportunities to practise regulation of aggressive behaviours.

Of course, rough and tumble play between young children can sometimes deteriorate and therefore adult supervision is vital. Rather than prohibiting the play, adults can encourage children to follow overarching rules of respecting and taking care of one another; with clear boundaries in place, this play can support children's health, wellbeing and holistic development.

Christine is a lead practitioner in the preschool room at a nursery in Scotland; we asked her about her approach to managing risky play at their setting.

We believe that it's really important to allow children to explore their environment and allow them to take some risks, and to challenge themselves and push their own limits. When it comes to outdoor play, like the climbing frame, it comes down to practitioners knowing the children really well, and knowing what they are capable of. We have one 3-year-old who is really agile, and he climbs straight up and over the monkey bars, we don't worry at all. Whereas, if another child tries to follow him, one of us will move a bit closer. We don't stop them from trying something, but we're there to supervise, but we always try to use positive language and encourage them to challenge themselves.

I think part of our role in keeping children safe is to help them understand risk, so we light fires in the fire pit, and toast marshmallows, but the children are always supervised, and we talk about fire safety.

When it comes to rough and tumble – well sometimes a group of children will have a bit of a 'pile-on' on the carpet, where they seem to like rolling into each other, so we just let them get on with it, but when it looks like fighting, even if they are just playing, we usually redirect them – we're not so comfortable with that.

As Christine explains, keeping children safe is a key priority; however, it is important to reflect on our responses to children's risky play. If we constantly tell children to be careful, that they might fall or they might get hurt, we can create anxiety about physical play. By taking a balanced approach, practitioners can help children learn to assess and manage risk, and benefit from the broad learning potential of physical play. The final part of this chapter will discuss how parents and practitioners can create opportunities for physical play in both indoor and outdoor spaces.

 TIME TO REFLECT

Take a moment to reflect on Christine's perspectives and practices at her setting, and how they compare with your own. How comfortable do you feel when children are using climbing equipment or using tools such as scissors? Think about the language you use most frequently during risky play – do you often tell children to be careful or do you tell them they are going to fall or get hurt? If so, are there ways you could adapt your language to encourage children to assess the risks with you?

What is your attitude towards rough and tumble play? If you are a practitioner, have you ever discussed rough and tumble play with colleagues or parents to agree your setting's position and approach to managing this type of play?

Creating environments for physical play

Young children's levels of physical activity and the range of movement they experience is dependent on the affordances of the environments in which they spend most time. Most young children are naturally active; however, it is often adults who arrange the environment, especially indoors, and control how children can move. Creating early learning environments that promote holistic development through physically active play does not require expensive equipment or specialist instructors; but it does need adults who appreciate the importance of movement and who have positive attitudes toward physical activity. Young children like to imitate adults, so where possible, they need physically active role models. Seeing their parents and carers enjoying physical activity will help promote enthusiasm for movement and exercise.

Physical activity needs to be thought of as an integral part of daily life, and there are many everyday opportunities to enable children to be active and move freely. However, this section explores some specific ways to promote movement and coordination through play activities at home or in early childhood settings.

Floor time

Many families live busy lives and some young babies spend considerable time in car seats and bouncing chairs; whilst these are very convenient, they can restrict babies' movements. Spending time on the floor, especially with their carer, promotes a range of movement. When lying on their back, babies lift their legs and grasp their feet; in doing so, they develop proprioception and they strengthen their abdominal muscles. Spending time in 'prone position', that is, on their tummies, strengthens muscles in the back, neck and arms. Placing a few toys nearby encourages babies to focus their vision and begin to reach and grasp objects. Some babies are not comfortable in prone position straight away, and very young babies might feel safer lying on their carer's chest, before gradually moving to the floor. As their strength and control develops, babies learn to roll from their front to their back, and vice versa. The World Health Organisation (2019) recommends that babies who are not yet mobile should spend 30 minutes a day in prone position (tummy time), spread throughout the day whilst awake.

Different spaces to move

It stands to reason that children need space to move; some spaces allow for vigorous physical activity and other spaces require more controlled movement. What is important is that babies and children have opportunities throughout the day for many different types of movement, including rolling, crawling, walking and running, jumping, balancing, climbing, throwing, catching and kicking.

Creating such spaces indoors might involve moving furniture to the sides of a room to allow for unobstructed movement or making a hallway or corridor a place for play. In the outdoor environment, big open spaces not only promote energetic movement, but they also allow children to gain a different perspective of their own body in space. It is also important that young children experience movement on a variety of surfaces, such as grass, sand, pebbles, woodchip as well as carpet, concrete and playground 'soft surfaces'. Different terrains, with uneven or unpredictable surfaces and gradients, provide different 'sensory feedback' to develop balance, self-awareness, and control (White, 2015). This is further enhanced when children can go barefoot on grass or sand.

Music, rhythm, dance and movement

Playing some music is a simple way to encourage movement; children naturally tune-in to a rhythm, and often respond with repetitive actions and movements that correspond to the music's tempo, such as bouncing, arm movements or jumping. Children's spontaneous dance moves often reflect the emotion and feeling of the music. This ability to coordinate rhythmic movement with an external beat is known as 'beat synchronization', which is thought to have many developmental benefits for young children, such as enhancing attention, language processing and self-regulation, amongst other things (Williams, 2018).

Nursery rhymes and songs with actions, such as 'The wheels on the bus', 'Wind the bobbin up' or 'One finger, one thumb keep moving', are an excellent way to develop both fine and gross motor control; and of course, these activities are excellent for encouraging language and communication, and social and emotional development. Musical games that involve 'stop–start', such as musical statues, help children to control their movement in response to sounds; for toddlers and young children, stopping moving and staying still can take as much physical control as starting to move.

Pushing, pulling, lifting, steering

Young children like to transport things; sometimes there is a reason for taking objects from one place to another; at other times, it is just part of the play. It is particularly noticeable in settings that embrace free play with open-ended resources, that is, objects and materials that children can use to develop their play according to their own ideas and goals, rather than the play being dictated by the materials (Änggård, 2011). Providing a variety of objects to transport, especially large heavy objects (wooden blocks, pebbles or old tyres) along with containers (buckets or baskets) provides opportunities for pushing, pulling and lifting. Not only is this play physically demanding, it develops children's understanding of concepts, such as size, weight, shape, volume and capacity.

Wheeled vehicles offer further scope for children to transport objects, as well as themselves and each other. Tricycles, dolls prams, ride-on toys, push-along toys or wheelbarrows all require children to develop spatial awareness that extends beyond their own body; they need to coordinate their movement with that of the vehicle. With opportunity for lots of different experiences, children learn how the vehicle moves differently on different surfaces, such as grass or tarmac, or on a slope, and they discover how to adapt their own movement and the force required in response.

Sand, water, mud and malleable materials

Play with sand, water, mud and malleable materials has immeasurable potential to promote children's physical and holistic development. When children play with these materials, they engage their senses and use their bodies in different ways. Large outdoor sandpits or digging plots, along with buckets, spades, rakes and wheelbarrows encourage a range of gross motor movements. When damp, sand and mud become heavy, which adds weight and resistance, requiring additional physical exertion. Indoors, sand and water trays with a range of bottles and containers, jugs, funnels, sieves, scoops and spoons promote fine motor control, hand–eye co-ordination and a multisensory play experience.

Play with playdough or clay is a very therapeutic sensory experience; it encourages children to use hand movements such as squeezing, squashing, pinching, flattening, rolling, poking and kneading. These actions develop muscle control in the fingers, hands, wrists and arms, that are required for holding and controlling a pen, or other tools. Adding plastic cutlery, scissors, rolling pins and shape cutters, for example, offers further opportunity for movement. There is no right or wrong way to play with clay and playdough, meaning that it is a highly creative activity, children can create sculptures or engage in imaginary role play.

Mark-making

Before children learn to write or create recognisable drawings, they enjoy making marks just for the joy of the movement and seeing the resulting marks appear. Providing large drawing surfaces with chunky crayons, chalk or paint brushes enables children to use gross motor movements; as their experience grows, they will gradually develop the fine motor control needed to form recognisable shapes, letters or numbers. Vertical surfaces, such as painting easels or blackboards, encourage large whole-arm movement, incorporating up and down, side-to-side and circular actions. In the warmer weather, you might give children large paint brushes, or rollers with a bucket of water to paint on outside walls or the playground. Similarly, spray bottles with water are great fun and develop the muscles in the hand and wrist.

These activities are just some of the ways in which parents and practitioners can enhance play environments that encourage children's physical and holistic development. They do not require expensive or specialist equipment; they make use of resources that are already available in homes, early years settings and the local community.

TIME TO REFLECT

Spend a moment thinking about your own activity around children and the messages you send. How frequently do children see you participating in vigorous physical activity, and more importantly, when they do see you being active, are you seen to be having fun and enjoying yourself? When caring for children in outdoor spaces, are you mostly active and involved in the play, or do you mostly stand back and supervise?

Concluding thoughts

Previous chapters have stressed how important it is for babies and young children to get the recommended levels of physical activity each day, and to develop a wide range of movement skills. Play comes naturally to children; it involves a diverse range of fun and engaging pursuits that increase activity levels and promote children's physical and holistic development, and their wellbeing, in many ways, so it is important for children to have access to a wide range of play opportunities. However, children's play can be enhanced or constrained by their environments, and by the perspectives of the adults who care for them. Children need spaces to move and play, and they need some opportunities to take risks. Expensive toys and equipment are not needed; everyday materials such as cardboard boxes and old sheets over chairs can be used to make obstacle courses, and old pans and crockery make excellent sand toys. By reflecting on our own attitudes toward physical play and adopting a sensible approach to risky play and rough and tumble, we can help children to assess and manage risk. Activities such as swimming, football or dance lessons also have a role in children's development; however, rich opportunities for physically active play can be created every day by making a few changes to the environment and making use of community spaces. Yet, one of the greatest influences on children's ongoing engagement with exercise is the attitudes of parents and carers. Lifelong positive attitudes are nurtured when children experience adults enthusiastically enjoying physical activity.

Top tips

- **Be a role model:** show children that being physically active is fun and let them see you taking care of your own wellbeing.
- **Provide a wide range of play opportunities**: review your environment to ensure children can engage in multiple different play types.
- **Mind your language**: think about the messages your words convey about physically active play, do you promote confidence or fear?
- **Involve children in risk assessment**: encourage children to consider the risks involved in different types of play and how to keep themselves safe.
- **Make space**: whether it's making interesting spaces for tummy time, or for crawling, jumping, dancing and so forth, adapt the environment throughout the day so that children have different spaces to play.

Key terms

'Taxonomy' of play	A taxonomy describes the practice of categorising and classifying something.
Open-ended resources	Toys and objects that can be played with in multiple different ways.
Attachment	The close emotional bond between babies / children and their caregiver.
Empowerment	Describes the process of babies and young children developing greater control over their own lives.
Self-efficacy	A child's belief in their capability to do what is needed to achieve their goals.
Prone position	A term to describe lying face down on the stomach, or tummy.
Beat synchronization	The ability to coordinate rhythmic movement with an external beat.
Spatial awareness	Being aware of one's own position in relation to the surroundings.

Further reading

Hanscom, A. J. (2016) *Balanced and Barefoot: How Unrestricted Outdoor Play Makes for Strong, Confident and Capable Children.* Oakland, CA.: New Harbinger Publications.

Scottish Government (2020) *Out to Play – Creating Outdoor Play Experiences for Children: Practical Guidance.* Available at: https://www.gov.scot/publications/out-play-practical-guidance-creating-outdoor-play-experiences-children/

UNICEF / Lego Foundation (2018) *Learning through Play: Strengthening Learning through Play in Early Childhood Education Programs.* Available at: https://www.unicef.org/sites/default/files/2018-12/UNICEF-Lego-Foundation-Learning-through-Play.pdf

References

Änggård, E. (2011) 'Children's gendered and non-gendered play in natural spaces', *Children, Youth, & Environments*, 21(2), 5–33.

Boundy, L., Cameron-Faulkner, T. and Theakston, A. (2018) 'Intention or attention before pointing: Do infants' early holdout gestures reflect evidence of a declarative motive?' *Infancy*, 24(2), 228–248,

Canning, N. (2020) *Children's Empowerment in Play.* London: Routledge.

Fleer, M. (2021) 'Conceptual playworlds: The role of imagination in play and learning', *Early Years*, 41(4), pp. 353–364.

Hughes, B. (2002) *A Playworker's Taxonomy of Play Types* (2nd edn). London: PlayLink.

Jarvis, P. (2007) 'Monsters, magic and Mr Psycho: A biocultural approach to rough and tumble play in the early years of primary school', *Early Years*, Routledge, 27(2), pp. 171–188.

Kress, G. (2009). *Multimodality: A Social Semiotic Approach to Contemporary Communication*. Abingdon: Routledge.

Lindon, J. (2011) *Too Safe for Their Own Good? Helping Children Learn about Risk and Life Skills*. London: National Children's Bureau.

Little, H. (2017) 'Promoting risk-taking and physically challenging play in Australian early childhood settings in a changing regulatory environment', *Journal of Early Childhood Research*, 15(1), 83–98.

McConnon, L. (2016) *Developing Young Children's Creativity: Possibility Thinking in the Early Years*. London: UCL – IOU Press.

Mountain, J. (2017). *Outdoors and Active*. London: Early Education.

Play England (2020) *Charter for Play*. Available at: www.playengland.org.uk/charter-for-play (Accessed 14th March 2023.)

Sandseter, E., Sando, O. and Kleppe, R. (2021) 'Associations between children's risky play and ECEC outdoor play spaces and materials', *International Journal of Environmental Research and Public Health*, 18, 3354. doi:10.3390/ijerph18073354

Solly, K. (2015) *Risk, Challenge and Adventure in the Early Years: A Practical Guide to Exploring and Extending Learning Outdoors*. Abingdon: Routledge.

Storli, R. and Sandseter, E. (2015) Preschool teachers' perceptions of children's rough-and-tumble play (R&T) in indoor and outdoor environments, *Early Child Development and Care*, 185:11–12, 1995–2009, doi:10.1080/03004430.2015.102839

Tremblay, M., Gray, C. Babcock, S. Barnes, J. Bradstreet, C. Carr, D. et al. (2015) 'Position statement on active outdoor play', *International Journal of Environmental Research and Public Health*, 12, 6475–505.

UNICEF UK. (1989). The United Nations Convention on the Rights of the Child. https://downloads.unicef.org.uk/wp (Accessed 14th March 2023.)

White, J. (2015) *Every Child a Mover*. London: British Association for Early Childhood Education.

Williams, K. (2018) 'Moving to the beat: Using music, rhythm, and movement to enhance self-regulation in early childhood classrooms', *International Journal of Early Childhood*, 50(1), pp. 85–100.

World Health Organisation (2019) *Guidelines on Physical Activity, Sedentary Behaviour and Sleep for Children under 5 Years of Age.* Geneva: World Health Organization. Available at: https://apps.who .int/iris/handle/10665/311664 (Accessed, 14th March 2023.)

Health and physical development

Jackie Musgrave

Introduction

Around 20 per cent of children have an additional need, such as a health condition, a special educational need or mobility difficulties, so it is important that such needs are examined to find ways to support physical development as well as making physical activity as inclusive as possible. This chapter will explore how conditions such as asthma, sickle cell disease and diabetes can be a barrier to full participation, but importantly, it will include knowledge about steps that can be taken to overcome such barriers. The content will also explain the link between physical activity and mental health and wellbeing.

By the end of this chapter, you will be able to:

- Identify some health conditions that can impact on children's ability to take part in physical activity.
- Consider some of the causes of childhood obesity.
- Explore the role of practitioners in relation to including children with additional considerations in physical activity.

Health conditions and physical development

Health is something that is often only thought about when we are feeling unwell and unhealthy. Think about how you feel when you have a bad cold, probably lacking in energy, headachy, hot and less motivated to do physical activities. And then, as soon as the cold goes away and energy levels return

DOI: 10.4324/9781003386728-6

to normal, we start to feel healthy and have more energy and can return to doing things without feeling exhausted.

Many children have a health condition that makes them feel unwell or lacking in energy for a lot of the time. The presence of such a condition can make it less easy to take part in physical activity, and this in turn can impact on their physical development and their sense of wellbeing.

The health conditions that are discussed in this chapter include:

- Chronic health conditions such as asthma, diabetes or sickle cell anaemia
- Special educational needs and disability
- Complex medical needs
- Obesity or being overweight
- Physical activity and mental health

The following sections look at each of these conditions, explaining how they impact on physical activity and development.

Chronic health conditions

A chronic health condition is one that is ongoing, lasting for three months or more.

Health conditions are characterised by symptoms, meaning features that are an indication that a condition or disease is present. For example, a child with asthma may experience shortness of breath and/or wheeziness. Many chronic conditions can't be cured, but the effect of the symptoms can be reduced by giving medication or avoiding some situations.

When a child has a chronic health condition, it is important that there is good communication between parents and carers with professionals who care and educate children. To help achieve good communication, in England, an Education Health Care Plan needs to be written with the parents' input. Taking part in physical activity requires consideration for many chronic health conditions.

Here are some of the most common chronic conditions that affect children in high income countries such as the UK.

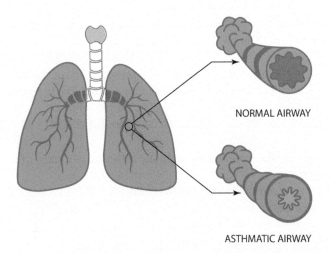

NORMAL AIRWAY

ASTHMATIC AIRWAY

Figure 6.1 Diagram showing a normal airway and an airway affected by asthma

Asthma is a common condition affecting between 10 to 20 per cent of children. Asthma symptoms include shortness of breath, wheezing and a night cough. Asthma often runs in families; it is not a condition that we 'grow out of' but it is typical for children to be diagnosed with asthma and for the symptoms to reduce or disappear for years, possibly returning in later life.

Asthma is frequently associated with allergy. It's not unusual for a child to have asthma, eczema, allergic rhinitis (inflammation of the nose causing it to run) and an allergy to a food product or to latex or pollen.

Asthma is a serious lung condition. In 2017, 17 children in England died following an asthma attack (Royal College of Child Health and Paediatrics, 2017). However, for the majority of children, asthma symptoms can be controlled.

The symptoms of asthma can be reduced by taking medication; these can by orally or via an inhaler. Inhaler medication goes straight to the lungs and so can work very effectively. Inhaler medication can be a 'preventer' which, as the description suggests, prevents symptoms breaking through. It needs to be taken regularly, usually twice a day, to reduce the inflammation and irritation in the lungs. The 'reliever' inhaler is intended to be used when asthma symptoms have been provoked by breathing in dust or a common cold virus. If the child is receiving the correct amount of preventer medication, the reliever inhaler shouldn't be needed on a regular basis. If a reliever inhaler is needed more than three times a week, it is an indication that asthma symptoms are not as well-controlled as they could be.

As well as being associated with allergy, asthma symptoms can be triggered by exercise and by cold air. This can be a source of anxiety to adults. On one hand, exercise is vitally important for children's mental and physical health and development (Asthma and Lung UK, 2023), but on the other hand, running around on a cold day can make a child with asthma wheezy, short of breath and may even trigger an asthma attack. Therefore, it's important to consider how children with asthma can be physically active, especially outdoors on a cold day, without provoking asthma symptoms.

CASE STUDY

Ollie, a child with asthma

The following case study looks at how Paramjit plans for Ollie, who is 3 and a half and has recently been diagnosed with asthma.

As you read the case study make notes about your responses to the following question:

> What do you think Paramjit needs to do to ensure that she is doing all she can to reduce the risk of Ollie becoming wheezy and/or having an asthma attack?

Ollie was diagnosed with asthma after having an attack that required hospital care. He has been prescribed a 'preventer' inhaler that he takes twice a day at home. However, Ollie also has a 'reliever' inhaler because, despite taking regular preventers, he occasionally gets very wheezy when running around, especially outdoors.

Paramjit has met with Ollie's parents, and they have written an Education and Health Care Plan, and Paramjit has learned how to administer his inhaler.

It's a sunny but very cold winter morning and the children are getting ready to go outside. What are your thoughts about what Paramjit needs to do to protect Ollie?

Comment

You may have considered the following:

Ollie should wear a scarf or snood over his mouth; this helps to warm the air before it enters his lungs and can reduce the risk of triggering his symptoms.

Paramjit should check the care plan to see what triggers Ollie's asthma. When Paramjit met with Ollie's parents, they discussed what triggered Ollie's asthma symptoms, and cold weather and physical activity were highlighted as being particularly triggering. When Paramjit checked the plan, she remembered that the parents had passed on the suggestion from Ollie's doctor that one way to reduce the risk was to give a puff of the 'reliever' inhaler before going outside.

Paramjit should keep a close eye on Ollie to ensure that he is not showing symptoms of asthma. She should be aware of the actions to take if he does; he may need to be encouraged to slow down or return indoors.

Diabetes mellitus is a serious condition that is becoming more prevalent (Diabetes UK, n.d.). There are two types of diabetes: Type 1 and Type 2. 96 per cent of children with diabetes will have Type 1. Type 2 diabetes is often associated with people over the age of 40, however, the number of children with Type 2 diabetes is increasing. Insulin is a hormone, or chemical messenger, that is produced in the pancreas; people with diabetes don't produce enough insulin. Insulin is required to regulate the level of sugar in the body and when the body doesn't produce adequate amounts, an injection of insulin is required to regulate the level of sugar in the body. As with all children, it is important that children with diabetes are encouraged to take part in physical activity, but there are many considerations to take into account.

Sugar levels are affected by the amount of sugar or carbohydrate that is eaten. The more sugar or carbohydrate eaten, the more insulin is required.

Another factor that can impact the balance between sugar and insulin intake, is the amount of physical activity undertaken. Sugar levels in the body can go down when physical activity is taken.

As the management of diabetes relies on achieving the right balance between carbohydrate intake, insulin dose taken in and level of physical activity, practitioners will need a great deal of knowledge about the condition so that children can safely be included in physical activity. In the following case study, Juwairiya, a practitioner working in an early childhood education and care pre-school setting draws on her experience of working with children with diabetes.

CASE STUDY

Juwairiya – a practitioner's view of managing children with diabetes.

Providing physical activities for children who have diabetes has many advantages, such as controlling insulin levels, maintaining healthy blood sugar and lowering the risk of heart disease.

There are many factors to consider when ensuring a child who has diabetes takes part in physical activities.

An important element to consider is the child's nutrition. Ensuring the child has enough food before and after they take part in physical activity. This could include working with a health professional, such as a diabetes nurse and/or dietitian to learn about appropriate foods for the child to take before and after exercise and then monitoring their blood sugar levels through an app to ensure it does not dramatically decrease after taking part in physical activities. This would all need to be noted in the child's individual health care plan. The care plan would state what steps to take if the child's sugar levels have decreased or increased to the levels where action needs to be taken to return it to a level within normal limits. The care plan should be easily accessible, and every practitioner should be made aware of this.

Another element to consider is what the child's current physical level is. It's important to find a baseline of the child's ability which will support practitioners in increasing the child's physical activity which will have a positive impact on the child's physical health. By discussing with parents and the child's key worker what type of physical activities the child undertakes at home and at nursery to find a baseline. The practitioner's role is to provide activities which slowly increase the intensity of the activities. This can be implemented through simple monitoring by practitioners to closely observe the child's verbal and nonverbal signs to identify if the child needs to stop or be pushed further. This would be done in conjunction with parents' observations on the signs they have seen and the medical professionals' recommendations.

The final element to consider is a practitioner's knowledge and understanding of diabetes and the impact it can have on the body. Also, understanding key terminology such as ketones, high blood sugar levels, low blood sugar levels. This is imperative in case the child needs to be admitted into hospital and parents are unable to be there. The practitioner's knowledge becomes so crucial to the success of the child's health and well-being.

Comment

Juwairiya has illustrated in her case study the depth of understanding and knowledge about diabetes that she has acquired. She draws on her previous experience and conveys how important it is to know the needs of each individual child, as they are all unique. She explains the importance of having an education and health care plan that everybody in the setting has access to and uses. Juwairiya also describes working with other professionals, such as specialist nurses and dietitians to gather knowledge about diet and medical care. And finally, she highlights how good communication with parents helps to identify and plan for the needs of children with diabetes.

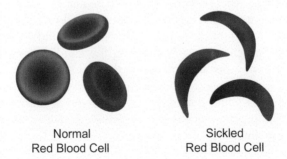

Normal
Red Blood Cell

Sickled
Red Blood Cell

Figure 6.2 Diagram to show difference between normal and sickle blood cells

You may have other thoughts about how practitioners can plan physical activity for children with diabetes.

Sickle cell disorder is a collective name for a series of serious inherited chronic conditions that can affect all systems of the body. Sickle cell anaemia is a sickle cell disorder. SCD is one of the most common genetic conditions in the world and affects around 1 in 2,000 of all babies born in England (Dyson 2016).

The red blood cells are an abnormal 'sickle' shape.

The abnormal shape of the blood cells means that as they travel around the body, instead of moving freely through the blood vessels, they can become 'stuck'. The accumulation of blood cells causes swelling and inflammation that causes pain.

Physical activity for children with SCD is challenging. Tiredness is common, and cold weather and vigorous activity can provoke a crisis. Advice to education settings that have a child with SCD is that they need to avoid changes of temperature and vigorous exercise.

TIME TO REFLECT

Consider children you are working with who have a chronic health condition. What considerations do you need to make to ensure they are included in physical activities?

The following section explores factors that need to be considered for children with special educational and/or complex medical needs.

Children with special educational needs may require additional support to encourage physical activity. Such support may include adapting an activity to make it more inclusive or having adult support to ensure safety and promote confidence.

Children diagnosed as autistic can benefit from physical activity because it can improve mood, coping skills and overall quality of life. However, it is often perceived that there are barriers to people taking part in physical activity. It is helpful for those leading on physical activities to understand how to make games and activities accessible to children diagnosed as autistic. For example, allowing for extra time for instructions to be processed may help

an autistic child understand what their role is, and may help greater participation. The National Autistic Society (2016) has published guidance aimed
at providing practical strategies to increase awareness and participation in
physical activity for autistic children; please see the link to guidance in the
further resources section at the end of the chapter.

Children with Attention Deficit Hyperactivity Disorder (ADHD) benefit
from exercise. The NHS offers the following guidance to parents of children
with ADHD: 'Make sure your child gets lots of physical activity during the
day. Walking, skipping and playing sport can help your child wear themselves out and improve their quality of sleep' (NHS, n.d.).

In February 2022, for the first time, government guidance was published
outlining the importance of providing physical activity opportunities for children with disabilities and special educational needs (Department of Health
and Social Care, 2022).

Children with complex medical needs can have difficulties with physical activity and with their level of development. Children can have complex
medical needs caused by a range of different factors. They may have experienced trauma, either during birth or afterwards, that may have caused a
brain injury resulting in the child having cerebral palsy. Or they may have
been born with a genetic condition.

Whatever the reason that a child has complex medical needs, it is often
the case that the condition has affected their physical growth and development. Their physical mobility is frequently affected, and they may even need
a wheelchair to move around. All of this can make taking part in physical
activity challenging.

An inquiry by the charity Sense in 2015 found that a child who has complex medical needs has fewer opportunities to take part in play activities in
early years settings. The findings revealed that the child's additional needs
were often perceived as a barrier to them being included in play activities.

An outcome of the inquiry was the publication of a toolkit designed for
use by practitioners in early education and care settings; please see details
about this publication at the end of the chapter.

Young children's mental health is a cause of concern, not just in the
UK, but globally. Children are increasingly being diagnosed with a mental
health condition. In 2017, the Royal College of Paediatrics and Child Health
(RCPCH 2017) reported that 10 per cent of children had a diagnosable mental health condition. Since the restrictions imposed to curtail the COVID-19

global pandemic, this number has increased. Part of the increase has been attributed to children not being able to attend their education and care settings because of closures. For children who live in housing and communities where there is limited access to outdoor spaces, this has had a disproportionately negative impact on their levels of physical activity and development. In 2019, the All-Parliamentary Party Group on a Fit and Healthy Childhood stated in a report that:

> In the context of improving children's mental health, it is important to recognise that mental health has a physical effect on the body and vice versa and that there is an increasing demand for emotionally stage-appropriate mental health and movement interventions in childhood.
>
> (APPG 2019, p 19)

The need to provide physical activity for babies and young children to improve mental health can easily be provided in early education settings, where outdoor play, physical activities and opportunities to move about are part of everyday routines.

Childhood obesity

According to the World Health Organization, 'overweight and obesity are defined as abnormal or excessive fat accumulation that may impair health' (2018).

Many children are an unhealthy weight and childhood obesity is a major health concern globally (World Health Organization, 2018). In England, one in five children are overweight when they start school and one in ten are obese. The increase in this number means that it is likely that many preschool settings have children who are overweight or obese.

Please read the case study of Ava, which focuses on a 4-year-old girl who is very overweight. The case study is included here to help develop understanding about why children become overweight as well as identifying ways of supporting the child and family.

The case study is followed by a series of responses for you to consider some ways in which you could support Ava and her family.

CASE STUDY

Ava – a child who is overweight

Ava is 4 and you have noticed that she is wearing clothes that are made for an 8-year-old; her leggings are rolled up because they are too long for her. You have also noticed that she is finding it difficult to get up off the floor and when playing outdoors, she becomes breathless very quickly.

Ava can't keep up with her friends' level of physical activity. She has started to spend her time with the adults in the outdoor area and is not playing with the other children.

Ava and her family live in an area of deprivation and living in poverty can have a profoundly negative influence on children's health (RCPCH, 2017). Ava is part of a big, loving family; she lives with four older sisters and their parents. Both parents come to pick her up from nursery and after giving her a hug, they put her in a buggy and give her a bag of sweets.

The nursery is located on a large housing estate in an area of high deprivation, with few shops and limited public transport. Most families on the estate live in poverty in low-quality housing, often with inadequate cooking facilities. There are three fast-food chain outlets that all offer cheap children's meals.

Questions

* Consider the reasons why you think Ava is overweight.
* What are your suggestions to address Ava's situation and work with her family?

Let's look at some of the reasons why children can become overweight or obese.

The child's environment

The really important point to take away from the case study of Ava is that she is part of a loving family, so her emotional environment will make a positive contribution to her wellbeing. Where a child lives can have an impact on the amount and type of physical activity that they can take part in. Living in a community where there is a high level of poverty can mean that there are fewer spaces for children to be active in outdoors.

Accessing nutritious food that's affordable is challenging because of the lack of supermarkets that sell high-quality food at prices that families who live in poverty can afford. Local shops are often more expensive and may not supply fresh fruit and vegetables. Leaving the estate to get to a discount supermarket can be difficult for many families. Public transport can be scarce, especially in rural areas.

Living in poverty is associated with poor housing and can mean that cooking facilities are limited. Low income can mean there is limited money to spend on gas or electricity and that can make cooking unaffordable within their limited means.

Low quality, high fat/sugar, highly processed foods are cheaper per calorie than higher quality, healthier foods – which often take more time and effort to prepare.

In relation to Ava, it may be that by giving her sweets, his parents are demonstrating their love for her in a way that is affordable.

Comment

The reasons why children become overweight and obese are complex. Despite many years of having what was referred to as an 'epidemic of childhood obesity' (Hall and Elliman, 2006, p. 179), finding solutions that work has proved difficult. However, as a practitioner in an early childhood education and care setting, you are well placed to help children who are obese or overweight. The following section looks at ways that you could approach Ava's parents about her weight.

Working with parents of children who are obese and overweight

Addressing a child's weight is a highly sensitive subject and many parents are unaware that their child is overweight (Public Health England, 2019). It is likely that they may feel shocked, angry, upset and guilty. Here are some suggestions of ways to work with parents of children who are overweight or obese to encourage more physical activity.

There aren't any easy solutions to addressing the many reasons why children can become overweight. Increasing the level of physical activity isn't necessarily the answer to reducing a child's weight, but for all the reasons discussed in this book, it is very important that all children are physically active.

However, children who are carrying extra weight can find it challenging to take part in physical activity. The reasons why this is the case is because carrying excess weight is hard work and it can be uncomfortable to move quickly; moving with excess weight can cause shortness of breath. To illustrate this point, imagine that you are running for a bus at the same time as carrying a bag of potatoes that weighs five pounds!

It is important to encourage physical activity for children like Ava and to work with her parents in sensitive ways. Consider the following suggestions.

Approaching Ava's parents

Ask to speak to Ava's parents and take them somewhere private to do so:

- Ask if they have concerns about her weight.
- Use sensitive language to explain concerns about Ava's weight.
- Explain that the aim for managing young children who are overweight is not to necessarily lose weight but not to gain any more, that is 'to grow into their weight'.
- Discuss ways of practitioners working with all members of the family to support Ava to increase her level of physical activity.

Working with Ava's parents

It is important to identify ways of incorporating physical activity into the normal daily routine rather than it being a special effort:

- Suggest that Ava is encouraged to walk some of the route to nursery.
- Think of ways to create opportunities and suggestions aimed at increasing the level of all children's physical activity so that Ava's parents don't feel singled out.
- Invite parents into the nursery to join in activities with their children.

Comment

You may have other thoughts about how you would approach Ava's parents about her obesity. In relation to children in your setting, you may need to take a different approach. However you approach parents about such a sensitive subject, the important things to bear in mind are the need for a gentle approach. It's also important to bear in mind the context of children's lives and the factors that may influence their weight. There may be little that you can do to change where a child lives and the amount of income available to the family, but you can review your practice to make your setting an environment that is likely to help children to reach a healthy weight.

Concluding thoughts

This chapter has outlined many of the considerations that are important to consider for babies and young children who have a health condition, and/ or additional medical or educational needs. Managing the impact of health conditions, special educational needs or complex medical conditions and/ or disability so that children can have opportunities to be physically active helps improve their mental health and wellbeing.

The following are some top tips for you to take away with you and put into practice.

Top tips

- Think about how you can work with parents in sensitive and realistic ways to support them to encourage their children to be physically active.

- Be prepared to learn about how to support children with additional needs to be physically active.
- Develop activities to encourage physical development that include all children and avoid making children feel any more different than they may already feel.
- Ensure that each child with an additional need that is affected by physical activity has an individual Education and Health Care Plan that is accessible to all staff.
- Learn about the conditions that affect the children in your setting and specifically the knowledge that you need to enable them to take part in physical activity.

Key terms

The table below gives definitions of some of the terms used in this chapter.

Term	Definition
Asthma	A chronic health condition affecting the respiratory system. The breathing tubes become inflamed, and this causes narrowing. The tubes produce excessive mucous. Common symptoms include shortness of breath, wheezing and a cough at night.
Attention deficit hyperactivity disorder (ADHD)	A group of conditions that can cause difficulties in attention and or concentration, impulsive behaviour and high levels of activity.
Autism	The term covers a range of different conditions that affect how people think and behave. There are some experiences that an autistic child may find difficult, such as social interaction; noises and sounds can be difficult to cope with.
Chronic health conditions	A chronic health condition is one that is ongoing and normally lasts for longer than three months. The symptoms can have an ongoing impact on everyday activities.
Complex medical needs	Children may have long-term medical needs as a result of injury, birth trauma or an inherited health condition. Their needs can include support with breathing, feeding, movement or toileting.

Diabetes mellitus	A chronic lifelong health condition where the levels of sugar in the blood go too high. There are two types of diabetes. Type 1 most commonly affects children, but there is an increasing number of children being diagnosed with Type 2.
Disability	Gov.uk states that, 'You're disabled under the Equality Act 2010 if you have a physical or mental impairment that has a "substantial" and "long-term" negative effect on your ability to do normal daily activities.'
Sickle cell anaemia	A chronic health condition that affects the red blood cells. Instead of being round, the cells affected by sickle cell disease become an abnormal shape, that looks like a sickle, a c-shaped farm instrument.
Special educational needs	Some health conditions can affect a child's ability to learn and additional support for their education may be required. Examples of conditions that may mean a child has special educational needs include attention deficit hyperactivity disorder (ADHD) or autism.

 Further reading

The National Autistic Society (2016) *Autism, Sport and Physical Activity.* Available at https://s2.chorus-mk.thirdlight.com/file/1573224908 /64485696828/width=-1/height=-1/format=-1/fit=scale/t=446198/e =never/k=0d813460/Autism-sport-physical-activity.pdf (Accessed 24 August 2023.)

Sickle Cell and Thalassaemia: A Guide to School Policy (available at: https://sicklecellsociety.org/wp-content/uploads/2015/01/Dyson -School-policy-sickle-cell.pdf) is a resource that you will find helpful to increase your knowledge about managing sickle cell in young children so that they can safely be encouraged to be physically active.

Sense: Resources for Education and Early Years Professionals. Available at: https://www.sense.org.uk/information-and-advice /for-professionals/resources-for-education-and-early-years -professionals/

References

All-Party Parliamentary Group (APPG) (2019) *A Report by the All-Party Parliamentary Group on a Fit and Healthy Childhood: Mental Health Through Movement* [online]. Available at: https://royalpa.co .uk/wp-content/uploads/2019/10/mentalhealththroughmovement _301019.pdf

Asthma and Lung UK (2023) *Help your Child Stay Active*. Available at: https://www.asthmaandlung.org.uk/conditions/asthma/child/life /active

Department of Health and Social Care (2022) *Guidance: Physical Activity Guidelines: Disabled Children and Disabled Young People*. Available at: https://www.gov.uk/government/publications/physical -activity-guidelines-disabled-children-and-disabled-young-people (Accessed 14 April 2023.)

Diabetes UK (n.d.) *Physical Activity and Your Child*. Available at https:// www.diabetes.org.uk/guide-to-diabetes/your-child-and-diabetes/ physical-activity (Accessed 14 April 2023.)

Dyson, S. (2016) *Sickle Cell and Thalassaemia: A Guide to School Policy*. Available at: https://sicklecellsociety.org/wp-content/uploads/2015 /01/Dyson-School-policy-sickle-cell.pdf (Accessed 24 March 2023.)

Equality Act 2010 (n.d.) Available at: https://www.gov.uk/definition -of-disability-under-equality-act-2010#:~:text=Definition%20of %20disability,normal%20daily%20activities (Accessed 11 December 2023.)

Hall, D. and Elliman, D. (2006) *Health for All Children*. Revised 4th edn. Oxford: Open University Press.

NHS (n.d.) *Living with Attention Deficit Hyperactivity Disorder*. Available at: https://www.nhs.uk/conditions/attention-deficit -hyperactivity-disorder-adhd/living-with/

Public Health England (2019) *National Child Measurement Programme: A Conversation Framework for Talking to Parents* [online]. Available at: https://tinyurl.com/y82h66bu

Royal College of Paediatrics and Child Health (RCPCH) (2020) *State of Child Health*. London: RCPCH. Available at: stateofchildhealth .rcpch.ac.uk

World Health Organization (2018) *Obesity and Overweight*. Available at: https://www.who.int/news-room/fact-sheets/detail/obesity-and -overweight

Putting it into practice

Introduction

The concluding chapter will continue the theme of how you, as practitioners, can put what you have hopefully learned from the messages in this book into practice. The chapter starts with a reminder of the role of adults in relation to role modelling positive behaviours about physical activity. It includes case studies from the different perspectives of adults and children; the case studies illustrate how everyday activities and routines can be adapted to support babies and children's physical development and to give them opportunities for physical activity. It includes a section summarising best practice in relation to working with parents. The chapter concludes with an audit that you can use to assess how well your setting promotes physical activity and supports physical development.

By the end of this chapter, you will be able to:

- Consider how physical activity and development can be supported with everyday activities and routines.
- Reflect on the role of adults in supporting physical activity and development.
- Assess how well your setting supports physical development and activity for babies and children in your setting.

DOI: 10.4324/9781003386728-7

The role of the adult: supporting children's physical development and promoting physical activity

A theme throughout the book has been to highlight the critical role that adults play in supporting babies and children to take part in physical activity as well as a role in enhancing their physical development. Here is a summary of some of the important ways that this role can be carried out:

- **Role-modelling:** Practitioners can have a powerful influence on parents' and children's views about physical development. One way of exerting this influence is for practitioners to role-model positive approaches to physical activity, showing enjoyment to children.
- **Starting with the child:** Identify activities that babies, and young children enjoy at nursery that are aimed at promoting physical development; ensure that you can adapt activities to meet the individual needs of all children.
- **Embed physical activity in routines**: Seek opportunities to encourage participation in everyday activities and consider the affordances of everyday equipment and activities.
- **Work with parents**: Share ideas with parents, let them know about the activities children enjoy in your setting and encourage parents to carry on doing them at home.

Manageable and accessible physical activity for all children

There are numerous factors that can impact how much physical activity children take and how they develop, some relating to health issues that we looked at in Chapter 6. Whatever the individual needs of the child are, ways to promote physical activity need to be realistic, so that it becomes part of an enjoyable daily routine for children and their families.

Through embedding manageable and accessible daily physical activity for children in everyday activities and routines, opportunities to be active may become more sustainable. It is also important that practitioners are aware of barriers that may prevent children and their families from being physically active. It is vitally important to work with parents to achieve this goal.

Case studies

Here are eight case studies of children that illustrate how you can plan to include babies and children in physical activity across a range of ages in different situations.

As you read about the children, consider the following questions:

1. What are the key points that you can take away from these case studies?
2. What is your role as a practitioner?
3. What are the implications for all colleagues in your setting?

CASE STUDY 1

Ali and Nic, 3-year-olds – the affordances of everyday objects that can support physical development and activity

Kris is sorting out the recycling, separating the cardboard, paper and clean plastic containers ready to put in the different collection boxes. As they put the cereal boxes, yogurt pots, newspapers and other stuff into different piles Ali and Nic, who are three years old, come over and pick up some empty kitchen roll tubes from the cardboard pile. Ali holds theirs up to their eye to look through it like a telescope turning around and looking up and down. Nic waves theirs around like a magic wand, pointing it at up at the ceiling then swooping around to point it at the door. Kris starts to ask the children to put the tubes back on the pile, but then notices how they are using them to play and move around. This gives Kris an idea, and they decide to ask the children to explore what they can do with the rest of the recycling. They make balls out of scrunched up newspaper, build towers with empty boxes, jump onto yogurt pots to make them flat, make hats out of envelopes and put their feet into plastic food containers to slide around.

Comment

This example shows that supporting physical activity does not require any specific equipment or apparatus, children's fine and gross motor skills can be developed using everyday objects. Showing parents how they can use their recycling materials as an opportunity to encourage physical activity is an accessible way of embedding movement into everyday life.

Kris is tuned in to the children, and she is closely observing them to help her realise that everyday objects, that are low cost and readily available have affordances that can support the children's physical development and activity.

CASE STUDY 2

Ben, 13 months – a competent baby becoming a competent toddler

Ben (13 months) is becoming more and more confident at standing unaided and taking his first teetering steps. He crawls over the bark surface and pulls himself up to a small table which holds a water urn and a selection of children's cups. Isaac (24 months) arrives at the table, perhaps to help himself to a drink, and immediately becomes distracted by the fun he can have by filling then emptying the cups on the table, using his hands to spread the water to the edges. Ben begins to copy his movements and soon they are splashing and giggling with glee. A passing practitioner asks them firmly to stop as this is supposed to be drinking water. Isaac realises this fun is over, and it is time to find an alternative; he dashes off to find it. Ben begins to cry either because of the firmness of the practitioner's tone, because the fun is over, or his newfound friend has abandoned him. As he stands there, crying miserably, he looks around to see if anyone will come to comfort him. After approximately two minutes he realises that no-one else is concerned and that he needs to take action himself. He begins to walk, taking halting steps away from the table. An incline is in his path and I wonder how he will manage; he stops and starts, his arms stretched in front to balance, concentrating so hard that his sobs become less and less until he has forgotten he is crying. At the top of the slope is a small platform built of pallets; he drops to his knees and uses his hands to help himself climb on. At the back of the platform is a convenient handrail which he uses to pull himself up, and then hold on to, as he surveys the vast outdoor area full of young children. As he tightens his grip on the rail, he notices he can rattle it so that the platform shakes a little. He repeats this action several times until Kamal (30 months) is attracted by the sound and motion and comes over to inspect what is going on. He grabs the other side of the rail so that he is facing Ben and they begin to shake and rattle the rail together. This causes great hilarity and soon Ben is once again giggling with glee along with another new friend.

Comment

The above observation was made at an ECEC setting in England that promotes babies' and toddlers' engagement with the outdoors; the children spend most of the day outside and their indoor environment is provided by a collection of yurts. It is a great example of the type of learning that can occur in a thoughtfully designed outdoor space for young children. If we asked you to note down all the learning and development occurring for Ben, in this one simple snapshot of his day at the setting, you may have noted physical, emotional, sensory, confidence, science, maths, social, relationships, self-regulation, wellbeing, agency, concentration, problem solving. You may even have noted others. All this learning happens in an unplanned for activity, within a carefully planned environment full of knowledgeable, confident adults who know the difference between 'interacting and interfering' (Fisher, 2016).

CASE STUDY 3

Archie and Jamal, 4-year-olds – managing rough and tumble play

4-year-olds, Archie and Jamal are best of friends at nursery and spend much of their time in the outdoor area. Staff noticed that they frequently engaged in quite physical, rough and tumble play, sometimes also involving other children as well. They would chase and swing each other around, fall on top of one another or come together in a 'rugby scrum' style lock, and push each other until they both collapsed. They were often out of breath and the play was usually accompanied by laughter and shrieks of delight. Nonetheless, nursery staff tended to discourage them, commenting that someone was going to get hurt, and redirecting them to other play. However, after a few minutes, the physical play would start up again. It soon became clear that different staff had quite different attitudes towards this sort of play; some would stop them immediately, whilst others would only intervene if the play got too physical.

The situation was discussed at a staff meeting, where it was agreed that rather than stopping the play, some 'rules' needed to be set. It was also suggested that the children should be involved in making the rules.

When the rough and tumble play began the following day, staff asked Archie and Jamal how they could make sure everyone stayed safe. Together, they agreed that they would only 'play wrestle' on the grass, and that if someone shouted 'stop', they would let go immediately. Staff stayed close by to supervise, and if other children came to join in, they were encouraged to watch for a few moments whilst staff explained the rules before they got involved. Staff were pleasantly surprised at how well the children adhered to the rules and noted that further rules were frequently negotiated and agreed between them, without any adult input.

A few weeks later, Archie and Jamal's play moved on to other things and the rough and tumble rarely occurred. Reflecting on the situation, staff felt that allowing the play with agreed rules had been beneficial for children's social and emotional development and their physical development. It had been an opportunity to foster children's sense of empathy, responsibility and fair play.

Comment

The staff identified a need for a consistent approach to managing Archie and James's rough and tumble play. And they realised that it was important to be able to allow the boys to go through what turned out to be a phase. By including the boys in the decisions about when to stop, they gave them agency and the understanding that their views were being heard and responded to. The response to the rough and tumble play phase also supported other areas of development, such as their social skills and emotional needs.

CASE STUDY 4

Lila, 5 years old – a walk to school

Lila was a vibrant 5-year-old girl with boundless energy, yet her mornings were often spent sitting in the family car for an hour as her mum drove her and her older siblings to their schools. Her older siblings were dropped at secondary school before Lila was driven to her primary school. She longed to run and play, but her typical morning consisted of sitting at a desk doing phonics and reading activities until first break. Recognising the lack of physical activity Lila was getting across the week, one morning, Lila's mother decided to make a change. Instead of driving her all the way to school, they parked a few streets away and started walking the rest of the journey together. Lila was thrilled at the opportunity to stretch her legs and feel the fresh air on her face.

As they walked, Lila's mother pointed out different trees, buildings and any wildlife they spotted as they walked through the local park, and they often talked about what they were looking forward to that day. Lila listened intently, taking in new information and enjoying the sights and time with her mum.

When they arrived at school, Lila's mother encouraged her to run around on the playground with her friends before class started. Lila's cheeks turned pink, and her eyes sparkled as she ran, jumped, and played. As Lila walked into her classroom, she felt invigorated and ready to learn. She could already feel her mind buzzing with new ideas and enthusiasm she had for the activities the teacher had set up.

Over the next few weeks, Lila became more active. Her mother continued to park further away, and they would walk to school each morning. Sometimes her friends, and their parents, would also join her for the walk to school. Lila's teacher also began to incorporate more physical activities into the classroom, such as stretching and breathing exercises when the children seemed distracted. The desks were replaced with activity zones and break out spaces to work and play.

Lila's concentration in class improved and she began to feel more confident and engaged in school. She also had more energy throughout the day and felt better both physically and mentally.

Comment

Thanks to the small, yet impactful, changes in her routine, Lila's physical and academic development would have benefited from the increased amount of physical activity. She would have learned the importance of physical activity and the positive impact it could have on all aspects of life by engaging in this with her mum over the course of her primary school years if this pattern continued. Initiatives like a 'walking school bus' can allow young children an opportunity to add physical activity to the start and end of their school day – especially important if the nature of their classroom and approach from their teacher is limiting movement and physical activity. Small daily changes can have significant impact over the longer term. A 15-minute walk to school at the start and end of the day results in an additional 150 minutes across the school week and 98 hours across the 39 weeks of a school year!

CASE STUDY 5

Mia, 3 years old – minding our language

Mia was 3 years old. Her parents had enrolled her in the nursery, hoping that she would get the opportunity to explore and learn new things under the watchful eye of professionals while they were at work. As soon as Mia entered the play area, she was running around, and her eyes widened as she saw all the toys, balls, and other play equipment.

She tried to climb on the ladder to reach the slide when a new staff member came over to her and said, 'Mia, be careful! That ladder is too high for you.' Mia was startled and hesitated for a moment. She turned around and looked at the staff member who had just warned her. The staff member looked concerned as she continued to keep an eye on Mia.

With repeated episodes of the same phrase being used, Mia became hesitant and cautious. Every time she wanted to try something new, she looked back at the staff member to check whether it was too risky. As she climbed the ladder, crawled through the tunnel or walked on the wall, she kept second-guessing herself, her movements becoming slow and cautious. The staff member always seemed to be watching her, so Mia never felt entirely free to experiment and explore.

Over time, Mia stopped trying new things that posed some risk altogether. Her exploration became less risky, and her play became increasingly passive. She never pushed herself to climb higher, balance on walls or beams and was reluctant when other staff encouraged and tried to support her. As she grew up, Mia never felt confident in her abilities to take risks and overcome challenges. She found it difficult to cope with uncertain situations, the fear of failure or it being too risky always looming in her mind.

Comment

The staff member's well-meaning warnings about 'being careful' and avoiding risk-taking had limited Mia's opportunity to build her own self-awareness of risk and to manage the level of risk she was prepared to take on and embrace. Had she been given the space to take risks and manage them on her own, she would have learned valuable problem-solving and movement skills that would have served her well throughout her life allowing great levels of physical literacy and creative movement to develop.

CASE STUDY 6

Jade, 3 years old – planning physical activity for a child with additional needs

The following is an excerpt from an interview with Caitlin, the manager of a large nursery.

Jade has global development delay, and she has a heart condition, which has meant that she has spent a lot of her life in hospital. As a result of long stays and inactivity, Jade has reduced muscle tone. She absolutely adores the whizzy dizzy (a piece of apparatus designed to help the development of gross motor skills). She would go on it all day, every day, if anybody let her and we can really see the impact it's had on her. One of the advantages of the whizzy dizzy is that it can be used indoors, and this is important for Jade because the monkey bars and other large equipment is outdoor equipment and can't be brought indoors. Because Jade can't regulate her temperature, she can't be outside for very long. So, the cold impacts her quite quickly, therefore, she spends a lot of time inside. We also have a Pikler triangle, and we have an indoor side in the two year olds room and things like that. For her to be able to use the whizzy dizzy inside where she's warm has made a really big impact on her.

Comment

This is a fantastic example of how practitioners can provide indoor activities aimed at promoting physical development for a child with additional needs, and importantly who can't go outside in all weathers.

Summary to case studies

The case studies present a range of different situations, some of them highlighting how physical activity can be encouraged through everyday routines, as discussed in Chapter 2. Others highlight how practitioners may inadvertently discourage children from engaging with physical activity because of concerns about risk taking and children harming themselves, a theme in several chapters. The message in each of the case studies is that there is a great deal that practitioners can do to support physical development and increase activity. The skills of observation and knowledge of child development that underpin the theory of being an early educator are helpful tools to enable planning activities that maximise physical activity for babies and children. And the final case study of Jade reminds us of the need to consider the uniqueness of each child and what adaptations may need to be taken to make physical activity as accessible to all children as possible, as discussed in Chapter 6.

However, to have greater impact on children's approaches to physical activity it is important that you work with parents.

Working with parents

Working with parents to gain their cooperation and willingness to provide opportunities for physical activity is key, and in a similar way to all areas of practice, building positive relationships with parents and the families of the children is critical to success.

Communication with parents can include keeping them informed about their child's development, as well as giving them ideas for continuing physical activity at home. However, not all parents are able to provide opportunities for physical activity at home. The parents may be disabled, or they may be short of time. The family may live in accommodation with unfriendly neighbours who complain about children making a noise. The local environment may not have play areas, and even if it does, parents may be concerned about their children's safety. This is where it is really helpful to know your families and their individual situation. Understanding why some families may not be able to support their children's physical activity can help you to be sensitive and non-judgmental in your approach.

Figure 7.1 Not all families have access to well-equipped and safe outdoor play areas for their children

Many settings hold events that involve activities that promote physical activity and invite parents and carers to attend. Such events are especially important for families who may not have access to outdoor spaces or the resources that help to provide physical activity opportunities for their children.

A whole setting approach to physical activity

Developing a whole setting approach to look at the ways that you provide physical activities for babies and children will encourage everyone to be aware of their responsibilities and the role they can play in this critical area of children's development.

Ensuring that less experienced practitioners and students continue to develop their skills in observing children so that they understand the uniqueness of the children in their care. Observing and knowing their children will help them to learn about their likes and dislikes, as well as learning what adaptations they may need to make to include children with additional needs as much as possible.

A way of developing a whole setting approach is to write policies in collaboration with all practitioners that embed opportunities for physical activity. Take some time to discuss physical activity in staff meetings, as well as in day-to-day conversations to consider how you may make best use of the environment both inside and out all year round to help promote physical activity and make it part of the everyday routine.

How does your setting support babies' and children's physical activity?

Of course, all settings are different, and each child is unique, so there isn't a one size fits all approach to how you can support children's physical activity. So, it is important to think about how you can consider each baby or child and their family's needs, and how you can make the best of the environment that is available to you.

To help you do this, Table 7.1 is an audit that you may like to complete to help you think about the factors that can impact children's physical growth, development and levels of activity. Think of anything that you can change or improve in your practice, as well as thinking about potential barriers to doing so and possible solutions. You may want to share this with colleagues in your setting as a way of developing or enhancing a whole setting approach to supporting children's physical development and encouraging greater physical activity.

Top tips

- Consider how you can build in opportunities to increase physical activity into everyday routines.
- Remember the affordances of everyday objects that can support physical development and activity.
- Develop activities to encourage physical development that include all children and avoid making children feel any more different than they may already feel.
- Be prepared to learn about how to support children with additional needs to be physically active.
- Work with colleagues to develop policies that embed and promote physical activity.
- Complete the 'how you support the physical growth, development and activity of babies and young children audit' and discuss it with your colleagues to identify ways to change your practice.
- Think about how you can work with parents in sensitive and realistic ways to support them to encourage their children to be physically active.
- Remember that there isn't one single approach to how you can support children's physical activity because settings and children are different.

Table 7.1 Audit: how do you support the physical growth, development and activity of babies and young children?

Factors that can impact on physical growth, development and activity of babies and young children	yes	How/when do you do this?	Could this be changed or improved?	no	What are the barriers?	What are the solutions?
Clothing and footwear						
			Baby or Child			
Is the **baby** given opportunity to be barefoot?	yes	Babies and toddlers go barefoot on the grass in the summer	Consider ways of giving them opportunities to go barefoot all year round		Identifying activities that include opportunities for babies to be barefoot indoors	Ensure babies are warm enough when barefoot. Ensure babies are happy to be barefoot; some babies may need to be gently introduced to being barefoot if they are not used to it. Identify activities that babies like – e.g., painting that includes foot printing
Do babies have enough room in socks or clothing (such as babygrows) so that toes and feet are able to move freely?						
Is the child wearing the correct shoe size? Given opportunities to go barefoot? Provided with waterproof clothing for outdoor play?						

Factors that can impact on physical growth, development and activity of babies and young children	yes	How/when do you do this?	Could this be changed or improved?	no	What are the barriers?	What are the solutions?
Play Are babies and children given play opportunities that promote **fine motor skills?** **Gross motor skills?** **Multi-sensory play opportunities?** Given **access to the outdoors?**						
Additional needs Does the child have specific **likes or dislikes?** Or **complex medical needs?** Or **a health condition** that can affect physical activity?						

Factors that can impact on physical growth, development and activity of babies and young children	yes	How/when do you do this?	Could this be changed or improved?	no	What are the barriers?	What are the solutions?
			Adults			
Are you **knowledgeable** about children's likely stage of development?						
The amount of physical activity a child should take each day?						
Do you know the **child's interests?** Do you use this knowledge to plan activities to promote physical development that follow the baby/child's interests?						
Do you have knowledge about how to promote **physical literacy?**						
Do you promote a **culture of movement** in your setting?						
Risk and resilience: Do you give children the opportunity to take risks? Do you give **watchful encouragement** to children when they are taking risks?						

Factors that can impact on physical growth, development and activity of babies and young children	yes	How/when do you do this?	Could this be changed or improved?	no	What are the barriers?	What are the solutions?
How do you **work with parents** to promote children's physical development?						
Do your **policies** promote a culture of movement in your setting?						
Are you and your colleagues a **positive role model** for children? Are you physically active?						
Environment						
Does the **environment** allow children the opportunity for **big movements**: to crawl, run, jump, dance climb and roll?						
Does the environment allow children to have **opportunities for small movement**?						
Does the environment allow **risky play**?						

The audit above is designed to highlight some of the factors that can affect children's physical growth, development and activity. The columns ask you to think about how and when you do so and asks you to think of changes or improvements you could think about introducing. If there is something that you don't do, you are asked to think about barriers and solutions to improving your support to babies and young children in relation to the factor.

The first example is completed with some ideas of how you might approach giving babies the opportunity to go barefoot.

Further reading

Manners, L. (2019) *The Early Years Movement Handbook*. London: Jessica Kingsley Publishing.

Reference

Fisher, J. (2016). *Interacting or Interfering? Improving Interactions in the Early Years*. Maidenhead: Open University Press.

Index

Bold page numbers indicate tables, *italic* numbers indicate figures.

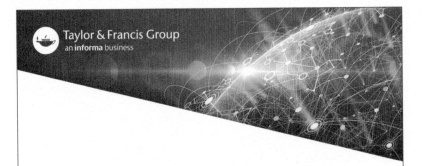